NICKNAMES

Ron Hauge and Sean Kelly

COLLIER BOOKS

Macmillan Publishing Company
New York

Collier Macmillan Publishers
London

MACMILLAN PUBLISHING COMPANY
866 Third Avenue, New York, N.Y. 10022
Collier Macmillan Canada, Inc.

Library of Congress Cataloging-in-Publication Data

Hauge, Ron.
Nicknames.

1. Nicknames. I. Kelly, Sean. II. Title.
CT108.H38   1987   929.9′7   86-31048
ISBN 0-02-040460-3

Macmillan books are available at special discounts for bulk purchases for sales promotions,
premiums, fund-raising, or educational use. For details, contact:

Special Sales Director
Macmillan Publishing Company
866 Third Avenue
New York, N.Y. 10022

10 9 8 7 6 5 4 3 2 1

Printed in the United States of America

The authors exhausted the patience and memories of many people in the course
(seven months) of researching this project. Special thanks to Jeff Christensen,
Warren Leight, Renée "Ol' Sleepy Hungry" Evans and Charlie "Bat-Bite" Rubin.

The following books were especially ransacked: *The Baseball Encyclopedia,*
ed. Reichler; *The Ring Record Book & Boxing Encyclopedia,* ed. Sugar; *20th Century American Nicknames,* ed. Urdang; *American Nicknames,* ed. Shankle; *The Dictionary of Historic Nicknames,* ed. Sifakis; *The Pseudonyms and Nicknames Dictionary,* ed. Mossman.

All mistakes, omissions, misspellings, and misattributions are, naturally, all our
fault.

CONTENTS

INFORMAL INTRODUCTION

A nickname is the hardest stone that the Devil can throw at a man.
—William Hazlitt, "On Nicknames" (1821)

If you please to compare the Roman names that sound so stately, because you understand them not, you will disdaine them in respect of our meanest names: for what is Fronto but Beetle-browed? Cassius but Cats-eyes? Petus but Pink-eyed? Cocles One eye, Naso Bottle-nose, Silo Ape's nose, Strabo Squint-eye, Flacuus Loll-ears, Labeo Blabber-lippe . . .
—Camden, *Remaines* (1605)

First Name First

Adam had no nickname. He had no last name. Just a Given Name, that is, the name he was given: Adamah ("out of the dust"). Of course, he had no Family Name. He had no family. Not even a belly button. Similarly, Eve was just plain Havvah ("life-giver").

One thing led to another, and they called the babies Cain, Abel, and Seth. And every newborn since has been assigned his or her own personal name.

Among the Jews, it is considered good form (and good luck) to bestow upon the child the name (or a variation of the name) of a venerable and dead ancestor. Catholics conventionally name a child at a christening, at which ceremony the tyke is stuck with the name of an officially canonized saint. (In France, even the civil law is very strict about which saintly *prenoms* are and are not permissible). WASPs tend to recycle Daddy's first name, and append Junior, II, III, etc.

The resolutely pure Puritans of the seventeenth century thought all that smacked of ancestor worship and idolatry, and endowed their chastely conceived offspring with first names like Prudence, Praisegod, Sufferanna, Increase, and Flee-fornication. Luckily, it was just a phase.

Nineteen-sixties hippies likewise rejected tradition, and named their flower children "Frodo Hopi Kyoko." Grace Slick of the Jefferson Airplane tagged her tad "god," had second thoughts, and renamed her "China." Abbie Hoffman begat "America," and Frank (Mother of Invention) Zappa fathered "Moon Unit."

Yuppies of the '80s prefer upscale corporate first names: "Kimberley" (presumably in honor of the highly profitable sanitary napkin concern) is popular, as is "Tiffany," with its expensive-collectible connotations.

But by and large, every Tom, Dick, and Harry is still called Tom, Dick, and Harry.

Last Name Last

As Adam's tribe increased, folks began to run out of suitable saint and ancestor names. So, to distinguish among the thousands of Johns, Ivans, and Patricks swarming around, the Surname was invented. (*Sur* is French for "on top of" or "also"). Often these surnames were Family Names, or Father-Names, aka Patronymics. So John became John Johnson, Ivan got to be Ivan Ivanovich, and Patrick was Patrick Fitzpatrick. Not much help there.

Next, geography was employed. A place of origin became a "cognomen," and thus many of us have inherited such last names as Hill, Dale, Meadows, Moore, London, Italiano (. . . even Hauge, which, we are given to understand, means "one who lives on a hill overlooking a cemetery" in Danish).

Sometimes a physical characteristic was cited to distinguish one John from another: Strong-arm John became John Armstrong, Little John became John Little, Brown John became John Brown. Kennedy, in Gaelic, means "ugly-shaped head" (and Fitzgerald means bastard son of Gerald— no wonder he called himself JFK).

Most frequently, a person's occupation was the source of his surname: we are descended from hunters, bakers, cooks, smiths, carters, farmers, and bishops (. . . Kelly, roughly translated from the Erse, means "cannon fodder").

Non-English-speaking immigrants to America were frequently assigned new Family Names by cretinous officials, and, as *Roots* readers know, *all* African arrivals were renamed, customarily with the Given Name of a

Roman statesman (Cicero, Cato, Marcus, Cassius) and the Surname of a Great American (Washington, Jefferson, Franklin, Clay). When Cassius Clay said he preferred "Muhammad Ali," it caused quite a stir.

Eke Names

"Eke" means (or rather *meant,* in Middle English) "also." By a linguistic process called "noncing," "an eke name" became "a nickname." (Similarly, a numpire became an umpire, a napron became an apron, a nunckle became an uncle. Go figure linguistics.)

A nickname, then, is an "also" name—in the same way that a surname is an "also" name. (Am I going too fast for you? You, in the back! Pay attention!)

So, for purposes of creating and applying nicknames, the old surname sources and traditions continued: place of origin (The Georgia Peach), occupation (The Railsplitter), and physical characteristics (Ol' Blue Eyes).

The big difference is that nicknames tend to be intensely personal, and therefore insulting, and therefore amusing. We create and employ nicknames to imply a certain *intimacy* with the person named: superstar, politician, family member, lover, co-worker, enemy . . .

To know someone's nickname is to know his or her secret identity. Secrets are taboo. Sex and violence are taboo. Some of the best nicknames are down and dirty.

For this reason (and the obvious commercial motives) we begin our survey with Sex and Violence nicknames—and not merely with the monikers of (allegedly) sexy and violent characters, but also with the nicknames of the tools of their trades . . .

1

THE BODY ECLECTIC

Pet Names Department

LOVE & SEX

You don't have to call me darlin', darlin', but you never even call me by my name.

—Steve "Chicago Shorty" Goodman

SEXY SADIE[1]   Maharishi Mahesh Yogi *(John Lennon's nickname for him)*
CUPID   Clarence Childs *2nd baseman 1890s*
LOVEBIRD   William F. Allen *politician*
AMERICA'S SWEETHEART   Mary Pickford (Gladys Smith) *actress*
THE VAMP   Theda Bara (Theodosia Goodman) *actress, aka "Queen of the Vampires," "The Original Glamour Girl"*
BABY VAMP   Mae "Diamond Lil" West *actress*
THE SEX KITTEN   Brigitte Bardot (Camille Javal) *actress*
AMERICA'S ANSWER TO BRIGITTE BARDOT   Lee Remick *actress*
THE MINX OF THE MOVIES   Betty Compson *actress*
THE SHAPE   Betty Grable (Elizabeth Grasle) *actress, wife of "The Kid" Jackie Coogan (1937–40) and "The Horn" Harry James (1943–65)*
THE DARLING   Amos Booth *utility infielder (1876–82)*
DARLING   Carling Bassett *tennis player*
BABY DOLL   William Jacobson *St. Louis Browns outfielder 1915–26*
HONEYBUNCH, BUNCH   Aline Kaminsky *cartoonist*
EASY   Ed Macauley *basketball Hall of Famer*
CHIPPIE   George Gaw *pitcher* / Bertha Hill *singer*
THE HAPPY HOOKER   Xaviera Hollander *author*
THE MAYFLOWER MADAM   Sydney Biddle Barrows *blueblood, former madam (alias Sheila Devin), author*

---

1. Sexy Sadie. John "Walrus" Lennon later apologized for chickening out and using a pseudonymous nickname for the priapic guru.

1

DEEP THROAT   *anonymous Watergate tipster*
THE VIRGIN QUEEN OF ENGLAND   Elizabeth I *reigned 1558–1603*
THE PLAYBOY PRINCE, RANDY ANDY   Prince Andrew *(now the duke of York)*
PLAYBOY[2]   Jimmy Walker *New York politician*
THE GREAT LOVER   Rudolph "The Sheik" Valentino (Rudolfo d'Antonguolla) *actor*
YOUNG CASANOVA   Hector Medina *fighter*
THE HE-HARLOT[3]   Warren "Winnie" Harding *29th president, aka "Bungalow-mind," married "The Duchess"*
THE FRESHEST MAN ON EARTH   Walter "Arlie" Latham *3rd baseman*
AVAILABLE   Sheldon Jones *Dodger pitcher 1946–52*
THE AVAILABLE MAN   (see "Canal Boy" James Garfield, U.S. President)
TOUJOURS PRET   (Always Ready) Porfirio Rubirosa *international playboy*
BEAU   George Bryan Brummell *British dandy, arbiter of taste*
BEAU JACK   Sidney Walker *lightweight champ 1942–43*
AMERICA'S BOYFRIEND   Charles "Buddy" Rogers *film star*
THE LITTLE MAN ON THE WEDDING CAKE   Thomas E. Dewey *N.Y. governor*
HUBBY   Husband E. Kimmel *U.S. admiral*
THE BACHELOR PRESIDENT   (see "Ten Cent" Jimmy Buchanan, U.S. Presidents)
WASHINGTON'S GAY YOUNG BACHELOR[4]   Jack Kennedy *(pre–Jackie O)*
STUD   George "Foghorn" Myatt *2nd baseman, manager, aka "Mercury"*
STUDS   Louis Terkel *writer, interviewer*
BUTCH CASSIDY   (Robert Parker) *outlaw*
MACHO   Hector Camacho *lightweight champ 1985*
HUNK   Heartley Anderson *football player, coach*
ADONIS   William Terry *pitcher, outfielder 1884–97*
THE NASHVILLE NARCISSUS   Charles "Red" Lucas *baseball double threat (pitched 157 wins, made 114 pinch hits)*
KISSING   Jim Folsom *Alabama governor*
KISSING BUG   Richmond Hobson *naval hero*
THE KISSING BANDIT   Morganna Cottrell *sports fan, publicity hound*
MR. KISS KISS BANG BANG[5]   Sean Connery *actor*
SMOOCHIE   Jerry Lee Smith *songwriter*
HICKIE   George Wilson *outfielder*
PINCH   Earl Kunz *pitcher*

2. Playboy Jimmy Walker, aka "Beau James," presided as mayor over a New York City rife with scandal and corruption, despite being, himself, a notorious heterosexual.

3. The He-Harlot. Someone is supposed to have observed to the pliable President Harding, "It's a good thing you weren't born a woman, Warren. You'd be in a family way all the time."

4. Washington's Gay Young Bachelor. Secret Service code-names for the two bimbos whom the married JFK liked to have on call were "Fiddle" and "Faddle."

5. Mr. Kiss Kiss Bang Bang. The Japanese call Connery this, because of his James Bond roles (according to Pauline Kael, who used it as a book title).

FOOTSIE   (see Head to Toe [Extremities])
HUG   Miller "Flea" Huggins *Yankee manager, aka "The Mighty Mite"*
CUDDLES   Clarence Marshall *pitcher*
SPOONER   Earl Oldham *songwriter*
RUBBER   Gene Krapp *pitcher*
MR. INSIDE   Felix Blanchard *football player* / MR. OUTSIDE   Glenn W. Davis
   football player
HUMP   Hubert H. Humphrey *LBJ's veep, aka "Pinky"*
PUMPSIE   Elijah Green *infielder 1959–63*
WHAM BAM   Steve Van Buren *football back, Hall of Famer*
WHOOPI Goldberg   (Caryn Johnson) *actress, comedian*
THREE-MINUTE   George Brumm *Pennsylvania politician*
CLIMAX   Clarence Blethen *relief pitcher (1923); record 0–0*
THE BIG O   (see The ABCs)
SKYROCKET   Samuel Smith *Louisville 1st baseman 1888, 1 home run*
DADDY OF THE BABY   (see "The Drunken Tailor" Andy Johnson, U.S. Presidents)
SPERM   Strom Thurmond *politician*
THE HONEY DRIPPER   Joe Liggins *saxophonist* / Roosevelt Sykes *blues pianist*
JACK THE DRIPPER   Jackson Pollock *abstract expressionist*
LOVIN' PUTTY   Julius Annixter *politician*
SLIPPERY DICK   Richard Connolly *19th-century New York politician*
DINK   (see Size)
JOHNNY WADD   John Holmes *porn actor*
10½ INCHES   Mark Stevens *porn actor*
RAMROD   Emmett Nelson *pitcher*
THE POCKET ROCKET   Henri Richard *Montreal hockey great*
THE LITTLE TEAPOT[6]   Henri de Toulouse-Lautrec *painter (visualize this one)*
DADDY WAGS   Leon Wagner *baseball great (visualize this one, too)*
BOLLICKY   Billy Taylor *pitcher 1881–87*
PUD   James Galvin *pitcher, Hall of Famer, aka "The Little Steam Engine"*
PUSSY, BEAVER   (see Mammals)
FLASH BEAVER   (Virgil Clifford West) *dancer*
COOZ   Bob Cousey *basketball player* / Jerry Koosman *pitcher*
TEETS   Sam Bataglia *criminal*
BOOB   Eric McNair *infielder 1929–42*
CHESTY   Lewis Puller *U.S. Marine general*
FANNY   Frances Kemble *author*
BUTTS   Albert Wagner *3rd baseman, brother of "The Flying Dutchman"*
BUM[7]   Oail Phillips *football coach*

6. The Little Tea Pot. Short and stout Toulouse-Lautrec's "handle" in the whorehouses of France. His ever-present erection was his spout.
7. Bum. In the U.K., "Bum" means backside. In the U.S., it means hobo. The U.K. word for hobo is "tramp," which in the U.S. means hooker.

BUGGER   Frank Welsh *football player*
KINKY   Richard "The Texas Jewboy" Friedman *country musician*
PEE MAN   Daryl Jones *fighter*
SMOKIN' JOE   (see Wood & Fire)
SLEEPIN' SAM   (see Attitudes)
CATO THE CENSOR   Cato the Elder *Roman moralist, d. 149 B.C.*

That Was No Lady Department

THE GIRLS

THE BETTY BOOP GIRL   Mae Questal *movie actress*
THE BOOP-OOP-A-DOOP GIRL   Helen Kane *singer*
THE BOX OFFICE GIRL   Gilda Grey *movie actress*
THE BLOOMER GIRL   Amelia Bloomer[1] *women's rights activist*
THE CHAMPAGNE GIRL   Trixie Friganza *vaudeville actress*
THE CHICKA BOOM-BOOM GIRL   Carmen Miranda *actress, aka "The Brazilian Bombshell"*
THE COCA-COLA GIRL   Jessica Dragonette *radio actress*
THE HUBBA-HUBBA GIRL   Vera Ralston *movie actress*
THE IT GIRL   Clara Bow *silent screen star, aka "The Redhead"*
THE MOON OVER THE MOUNTAIN GIRL   Kate Smith *aka "Song Bird of the South"*
THE O. HENRY GIRL   Agnes Ayres *movie actress*
THE OOMPH GIRL   Ann Sheridan *movie actress*
THE ORIGINAL BATHING GIRL   Vera Steadman *model*
THE ORIGINAL GLAMOUR GIRL   Theda Bara (see "Vamp," Love & Sex)
THE PEEK-A-BOO GIRL[2]   Veronica Lake (Constance Ockelman) *movie actress*
POOR LITTLE RICH GIRL   Barbara Hutton *heiress*
THE REBEL GIRL   Emma Goldman *revolutionary*
THE SARONG GIRL   Dorothy Lamour (Mary Leta Dorothy Kaumeyer) *actress*
THE SWEATER GIRL   Lana Turner (Julia Turner) *movie actress*
THE GIRL IN THE RED VELVET SWING   Evelyn Nesbit (see the movie *Ragtime*)
THE GIRL WITH THE GINGER SNAP NAME   ZaSu Pitts *actress*

1. Amelia Bloomer (1818–94) bravely gave her name to the commodious culottes she advocated so women could bicycle, among other things.
2. Peek-a-boo. Veronica Lake's "trademark" was long ash-blond hair spilling down wantonly over her left eye. During WWII she made the ultimate sacrifice, posing for pictures with her hair tied back, setting an example of industrial safety for every Rosie the Riveter.

SWEET EMMA THE BELL GAL   Emma Barrett *blues singer*
ALICE COOPER   Vincent Furnier *pop singer*
BRENDA   Mick Jagger *(to his fellow Rolling Stones)*

Boys Will Be Boys Department

THE BOYS

BIG BOY   Arthur Crudup[1] *blues singer* / Frank Goodie *tenor sax player*
BLIND BOY FULLER   (Allen Fulton) *bluesman*
BOY   Bryan (see "Silver Tongue," Head to Toe [Mouths]) / George (George O'-
Dowd) *British pop singer* / Dave Green *fighter*
BUDDY BOY   Walter Hawkins *blues guitarist*
BUTCHER BOY   Baer (see "Madcap Maxie," Attitudes)
GOLDEN BOY   Paul Hornung *Green Bay football great*
HONEY BOY   David Edwards *blues singer*
JUKE BOY   Weldon Bonner *singer, guitarist*
MEIN BOY[2]   Alex Levinsky *hockey player*
THE NEWSBOY   Abe Hollandersky *fighter (fought 1,309 fights)*
POP BOY   Clarence Smith *pitcher*
PRETTY BOY   Charles Arthur Floyd *gangster*
SCHOOLBOY   Lynwood Rowe, Hoyt Waite *pitchers*
SOLDIER BOY   George Curry *pitcher*
SONNY BOY WILLIAMSON   Aleck Miller (1899–1965), John Lee (1914–48) *blues
singers*
SUGAR BOY   Joseph "Po' Joe" Williams *singer*
THE TEXAS JEWBOY   (see "Kinky," Love & Sex)
WATER BOY   Major Peter W. Rainier *North Africa water supply chief, WWII*
THE BOY GENIUS   Orson Welles *filmmaker*
THE BOY MANAGER   Lou Boudreau *baseball manager*
THE BOY WONDER   Stanley Harris *baseball manager*
THE BEALE STREET BLUES BOY   B. B. King *guitarist, singer*
THE BOSTON STRONG BOY   John L. Sullivan *heavyweight champ 1882–92*
LITTLE BOY BLUE   (see Cartoon & Other Literary Figures)
BOYSCOUT   Bill Milliken *politician, aka "The Lollipop Governor"*

---

1. Big Boy Arthur Crudup has a better claim than most to the title "Father of Rock and
Roll."
2. Mein Boy. Levinsky was a rare bird indeed, a Jewish hockey player (for the Toronto
Maple Leafs, in the '30s).

The Bonehouse Department

HEAD TO TOE

The Body

THE BODY   Marie McDonald *movie actress*
SKINS   John Jones *baseball player*
BONES   Hugh Taylor *Redskins end 1947–54*
OLD BONES   Joe Brown *lightweight fighter* / Earl Morrall *football quarterback* / Exterminator *racehorse (1918 Kentucky Derby winner)*
THE SKULL   Charles Canhan *U.S. general*
MUSCLES[1]   Joe "Ducky Wucky" Medwick *baseball Hall of Famer*
MUSCLE   Leo Shoals *baseball player*
YUSSEL THE MUSCLE   Joe "We Wuz Robbed" Jacobs *fighter, fight manager*
JINGLE JOINTS   Ron Sellars *football end 1969–73*
SHOULDERS   Tom Acker *pitcher*
ELBOWS   Don Awry *hockey player* / George McFadden *fighter*
HORSE BELLY   Joe Sargent *Detroit Tiger 1921*
LEADBELLY   (Huddie Ledbetter) *blues singer*
ELVIS THE PELVIS   (see "The King," Assumed Titles)
DR. HIP   Eugene Schoenfield *medical columnist*
SNAKEHIPS   William Tucker *running back 1967–71*
TEETS, BUTTS, etc.   (see Love & Sex)
PARKYAKARKUS   Harry Einstein *radio comic, father of comedian Albert Brooks*

Heads

BASKETHEAD   Jean-Claude "Baby Doc" Duvalier *deposed Haitian "President for Life," son of "Papa Doc" (François)*
BIG BEEFHEAD   Cleveland (see "The Buffalo Hangman," Crime & Punishment)
BLOCKHEAD[2]   William Wordsworth *English poet, aka "Horseface," "Clownish Sycophant"*
BONEHEAD   Fred Merkle *baseball player, earned his nickname by erring in a World Series game*
BURRHEAD   Joe Dobson, Ferris Fain *pitcher and 1st baseman for 1953 White Sox*
CEMENTHEAD   Dave Semenko *hockey player*

1. Muscles. Joe Medwick, a National League outfielder for 17 years, was a fitness freak, and the walk it gave him inspired the "Ducky Wucky" slur. He entered the Baseball Hall of Fame as just plain "Ducky."

2. Blockhead. When he turned politically conservative, Wordsworth lost the respect of his fellow Romantics. His lengthy description of an intense poetic experience while out rowing (in *The Prelude*) got him called "The Little Man in the Boat."

CLEANHEAD   Eddie Vinson *jazz sax player*
DEADHEAD   J. O. Fernandez *Louisiana politician, aka "Coroner"*
FATHEAD   David Newman *jazz sax player*
MOTORHEAD   Jim Sherwood *musician (Mothers of Invention)*
PEAHEAD   Douglas C. Walker *football coach*
PUDDINGHEAD   Ed Battle *jazz musician*
PUDDIN' HEAD   Willie Jones *3rd baseman*
REDHEAD, OL' REDHEAD (see Hair)
SCHINOCEPHALUS (ONIONHEAD)   Pericles *Athenian statesman, d. 429 B.C.*
SNAKEHEAD   Charles Sheppard *rodeo rider*
SQUAREHEAD   Frank Finley *rodeo rider*
SQUIRREL HEAD   George B. Terrell *Texas politician*
TENNIS BALL HEAD   Steve Hovley *outfielder*
DEATH'S HEAD   Hermann von Hoth *German general, WWII*
HEAD HUNTER   F. Lee Bailey *attorney*

Faces

BABY FACE   Jimmy McLarnin *fighter* / George Nelson *gangster, aka "Public Enemy No. 2" (alias Lester M. Gillis)* / Jesse Thomas *bluesman*
THE GREAT STONEFACE   Ed Sullivan *television host*
HORSEFACE   (see "Blockhead," Heads)
LITTLE POKER FACE   Helen Wills *tennis champ*
THE MOON-FACED SENATOR FROM WORCESTER   George F. Hoar *Massachusetts politician*
OLD TOMATO FACE   Charles Leo "Gabby" Hartnett *Hall of Fame catcher*
PENITENTIARY FACE [3]   Jeffrey Leonard *S.F. Giants outfielder*
POKER FACE   John Nance Garner *vice president, 1933-41, aka "Mohair Jack," "The Owl," "Cactus Jack"*
STONEFACE   Joseph F. "Buster" Keaton *actor, filmmaker*
TOMATO FACE   Henry "Nick" Cullop *pitcher*
MAN OF 1,000 FACES   Lon Chaney *actor*
APPLE CHEEKS   Harry Lumley *hockey goaltender*
DIMPLES   Edward "Pop" Tate *catcher*
ZIT   (see Gimps)

Eyes, Vision

BANJO EYES, POP-EYES   Eddie Cantor (Edward Itzkowitz) *comedian-singer*
BIG EYE   Louis Nelson *jazz musician*
BIRD EYE   Harry Truby *2nd baseman 1895–96*

---

3. Penitentiary Face. When Mr. Leonard recently objected to this label, a New York sportswriting wag suggested "Correctional Institution Face" as an up-scale alternative.

BLANK-EYED DRAGON   Adrian De Wiart *British general (to the Chinese)*
CAMERA EYE   Max Bishop *A's 2nd baseman 1924–34, aka "Tilly"*
COCKEYE MULLIGAN   (David Albin) *racketeer*
DEADEYE DICK[4]   Nat Love *gunfighter*
EAGLE EYE   Jake Beckley *1st baseman 1888–1907 (Hall of Famer)*
EAGLE-EYED ERNIE   Earnest J. King *U.S. admiral*
THE ELECTRIC EYE   Flynn Robinson *basketball player*
THE HUMAN EYEBALL   Bristol Lord *baseball player*
OLD GIMLET EYE   Smedley D. Butler *U.S. Marine general, aka "Hell's Devil"*
OL' BLUE EYES   Frank "The Chairman of the Board" Sinatra *aka "The Voice,"* "Swoonatra"
POPEYE   William E. Simon *secretary of the treasury*
RED EYE   James Hay *hockey player*
FOUR EYES, TELESCOPE TEDDY   (see "Teddy" Roosevelt, U.S. Presidents)
SPECS   Joseph O'Keefe *Brinks robbery suspect* / Gordon Powell *drummer* / Billy Rigney *baseball player, aka "The Cricket"*
WINK   Winston Conrad Martindale *game show host, aka "The Winker"*
BLINKY   Frankie Palermo *gangster*
PEEK-A-BOO   William Veach *pitcher*
THE PEEK-A-BOO GIRL   Veronica Lake (Constance Ockelman) *movie actress*
WEEPING, CRYING   (see Attitudes)
THE LOOK   Lauren Bacall (Betty Joan Perske) *actress, aka "Windmill"*
OLIVER OPTIC   William Taylor Adams *writer*
EYECHART   Doug Gwosdz *catcher (named for his last name)*

Noses

OLD NOSEY   Arthur Wellesley, 1st Duke of Wellington *British general and statesman, aka "The Iron Duke"*
THE SCHNOZZ   Jimmy Durante *musician-comedian*
SCHNOZZ   Ernie Lombardi *Hall of Fame catcher, aka "Bocci"*
BUTTON NOSE   Jane Wyman *actress (to her ex Ronald Reagan)*
BANANA NOSE   Eddie Arcaro *jockey*
CHERRY NOSE   Charlie Gieo *mobster*
SKI NOSE[5]   Bob Hope (Leslie Townes Hope) *comedian*
BOOTNOSE   Sid Abel *hockey star* / Fred Hoffman *catcher*
BLUENOSE[6]   Norma Smith *poetess*

---

4. Deadeye Dick. Nat Love was an outlaw, mountain man, gunfighter, and sometimes Crow Indian chief. He was black.
5. Ski Nose. Hope boxed a while as "Packy East." He says he changed his stage name to Bob because "Les Hope" sounded like a judgment of his act.
6. Bluenose. Pseudonymous poetess Smith is not admitting to a puritan streak, but honoring a famous Nova Scotian racing vessel, the *Bluenose*.

BROWN NOSE OF THE YEAR   (see Attitudes)
BEAK   Danny Kravitz *catcher*
DUCK BILL   (see "Wild Bill," Attitudes)
PUG   Horace Allen *Brooklyn outfielder 1919 (4-game career)*
BOOGER RED   Thomas Norbis, Jr. *football player*

Mouths

BIG MOUTH   Martha Raye *actress*
GATEMOUTH   Clarence Brown *jazz singer*
MOTORMOUTH   Paul Blair *outfielder* / Andrew Young *diplomat, politician*
SATCHMO (SATCHEL MOUTH), DIPPER MOUTH, GATEMOUTH   (Daniel) Louis
    Armstrong *legendary singer and trumpet player, aka "Pops"; husband of*
    "Brown Sugar"
CHOPS   Siggy Broskie *catcher*
JAWS   Osvaldo Ocasio *fighter*
SQUARE JAW   Bill Ramsey *baseball player*
LEO THE LIP   Leo Durocher *shortstop (17 years), baseball manager (24 years)*
HOT LIPS   Henry Levine, Oran Page *trumpeters* / Hartley Edwards *WWI army*
    bugler
THE (LOUISVILLE) LIP[7]   Muhammad Ali (Cassius Clay, Jr.) *heavyweight champ*
    1964–70, 1974–78, 1978–79, aka "The Greatest"
SILVER TONGUE   William Jennings "Boy" Bryan *politician, orator, aka "The*
    Great Commoner," "The Great Orator"
WAGON TONGUE   Joe Adams *pitcher*
BLOWER   Lew Brown *pitcher*
LICK   Archibald "Alex" Malloy *pitcher*
DRIBBLE PUSS   Lew Lehr *spitting comedian*
TOBACCO CHEWIN' JOHNNY   Johnny Lanning *pitcher*
SPITTIN' BILL   Bill Doak *pitcher*
TOOEY[8]   Carl Spaatz *U.S. general, WWII*

Extremities

THE ARM   Tom Hafey *3rd baseman*
GLASS ARM   Eddie Brown *outfielder*
RUBBER ARM   George "Sarge" Connally *pitcher, aka "Rip and Snorter"*
THE MAN WITH THE GOLDEN ARM   Sandy Koufax *Dodger pitching great*
DADDY LONG ARMS   Don Contel *basketball player*

---

7. The Louisville Lip. Ali was also "The Mouth That Roared." He was, himself, a great
coiner of nicknames for his opponents: "The Big Ugly Bear," "The Rabbit," etc.
    8. Tooey. Spaatz combined with General Henry "Hap" Arnold and U.K. General Arthur
T. "Ginger" ("Bomber") Harris to do a number on Dresden.

SLOW HAND   Eric Clapton *guitarist*
BIG HANDS   Gary Johnson *football lineman*
IRON HANDS   Chuck Hiller *error-prone infielder*
STONE HANDS   Roberto Duran *lightweight champ 1972–78, welterweight champ 1980*
THUMBS   Kenneth Roy Carlisle *C&W performer*
GREASY THUMB JAKE   Jack Gusik *criminal accountant*
KNUCKSIE   Phil Niekro *knuckleball pitcher*
FINGERS JOE CARR   (Louis Bush) *pianist*
BUTTERFINGERS   Thomas R. Moran *pickpocket*
FAST FINGERS   Jimmy Dawkins *guitarist*
LEFTY[9]   William Frizzell *C&W great, once a southpaw fighter* / Vernon "Goofy" Gomez, Robert Grove *Hall of Fame pitchers* / etc.
LEFTY LOUIE   Louis Rosenberg *alias of the early 1900s hitman*
RINGO STARR   (Richard Starkey) *former Moptop with "The Fab Four"*
LEGS   Larry Smith *musician*
THE LEGS   Marlene Dietrich *actress*
LEGS DIAMOND   John Thomas Noland *criminal, aka "Diamond Jack," "Clay Pigeon"*
CRAZY LEGS   Elroy Hirsch *football back, Hall of Famer*
DADDY LONG LEGS   William McAdoo *secretary of the treasury, aka "Dancing Fool"*
PIANO LEGS   Charles Hickman *between 1897 and 1908 played 8 positions for 8 baseball teams*
BIRD LEGS   Willie Jensen *fighter*
RUBBERLEGS   Lee Guttero *basketball* / Roscoe Miller *pitcher* / Henry Williams (Williamson) *singer*
MUTTONLEG   Ted Donnelly *trombonist*
BABE RUTH'S LEGS[10]   Sammy Byrd *baseball player, golfer*
SHANKY JACK   Chiang Kai-shek *(to GIs)*
FOOTS   Walter Thomas *jazz musician*
FOOTSIE   Wayne Belardi *1st baseman*
FOOTSIES   Johnny Marcum *good-hitting pitcher 1933–39*
BIG FOOT   Dave Johnson *fighter* / Pete Ladd *pitcher*
BUCKET FOOT   Al Simmons *baseball slugger, aka "The Duke of Milwaukee"*
SLAMFOOT   Dan Minor *trombonist*
SLEWFOOT   Cecil Butler *pitcher*

9. Lefty. The last (and greatest) of pitchers answering to "Lefty" was Steve Carlton of the Phillies. (Only in plays by Clifford Odets is "Lefty" a political nickname.)
10. Babe Ruth's Legs. Late in the Bambino's illustrious career, Byrd would substitute for the rotund slugger on the basepaths and in the outfield. In 1935, when the Yankees traded Ruth to Boston, Byrd went to Cincinnati.

SUPERFOOT   Bill Wallace *high-kick karate champ*
PUSSY FOOT   William Eugene Johnson *G-man, "Untouchable"*
TURKEYFOOT   Frank Brower *1st baseman, outfielder*
DEERFOOT   Harry Bay *base-stealing outfielder*
DADDY HOOVES   Gus Gerard *basketball player*
BAREFOOT   Bobby Dews *minor league baseball prospect*
BOOTS   George Grantham *baseball player* / Henry Mussulli *sax player*
SHOE   Willie Shoemaker *jockey*
WHITE SHOES   Billy Johnson *football end*
SHOELESS   Joe Jackson *baseball immoral immortal* ("Say it ain't so!")
THE STOCKING-FOOT ORATOR (see McKinley, U.S. Presidents)
SILK STOCKING   Harry Schafer *3rd baseman (The Boston Red Stockings, 1870s)*
SOCKS   Harry Seibold *baseball player*
SOCKLESS   Jerry Simpson *Kansas politician*
SPATS   Leonard Moore *football player*
THE BAREFOOT BOY OF WALL STREET   Wendell Willkie *politician, industrialist*
JAY SILVERHEELS   (Harold Smith) *actor (Tonto)*
TWINKLETOES[11]   George Selkirk *Yankee outfielder*
TOE   Hector Blake *hockey player, coach, aka "The Old Lamplighter"*
THE TOE   Lou Groza *football placekicker*

Hair

FUZZ   Albert White *baseball player*
FUZZY   J. Forrest Knight *actor, musician* / Al Smith *baseball player* / Frank
   Zoeller *golfer*
FURRY   Walter Lewis *blues guitarist*
BUSHY GRAHAM   (Angelo Geraci) *Italian-born fighter*
NAPPY   Napoleon Brown, Hildon Lamare *musicians*
CURLY   Harry "Mr. Economy" Byrd *Virginia senator* / Joe Howard *Stooge*
KINKY   Richard "The Texas Jewboy" Friedman *country musician*
FRIZ   Isadore Freleng *animator*
THE BLOND BRUISER   Al Ettore *fighter*
THE BLOND BLIZZARD   Robert Fenimore *football player*
THE BLOND BOMBSHELL, PLATINUM BLOND   Jean Harlow (Harlean Carpenter)
   actress
THE REDHEAD   Clara Bow *silent screen star, aka "The It Girl"*
THE OL' REDHEAD   Walter "Red" Barber *sports announcer*
THE WHITE-HAIRED GUY   Joseph Gallo *crime consigliere*

11. Twinkletoes. George Selkirk took Ruth's place in the Yankee outfield, and, to judge
by his nickname, had legs of his own.

YELLOW HAIR   George Armstrong Custer *(to Indians)*
THE BEARD   Mitch Miller *sing-along bandleader*
BLACKBEARD   James Teach *murderer*
BLUEBEARD   Henry Desiré Landru *19th-century French wife killer*
REDBEARD   Frederick I *(of Prussia)*
PINK WHISKERS   Senator James H. Lewis *aka "Beau Brummel of the Senate,"* *"The Fashion Plate"*
ELECTRIC WHISKERS   General Bergonzoli *WWII (Italian)*
OL' STUBBLE BEARD, WIRE WHISKERS   Burleigh "Boiling Boily" Grimes *aka "The Senator," last of the spitball pitchers*
A NONENTITY WITH SIDE-WHISKERS   (See Chet Arthur, U.S. Presidents)
BEARDLESS[12]   Barbara Collins *journalist*
THE BOBBED HAIR BANDIT   Celia Cooney *Brooklyn bank robber*
PIGTAIL   Billy Riley *outfielder (1870s)*
PROFESSOR LONGHAIR   (Harold Roeland Byrd) *jazz pianist*
THE MOPTOPS   the Beatles *aka "The Fab Four"*
BALD   Billy Barnie *baseball manager*
BALDY   Mike Love[13] *Beach Boy* / Richard Rudolph *pitcher* / William F. Smith *Union general*
BALD COOT   Alexander I *czar of Russia*
BALD EAGLE   (see Birds)
THE BRUSH   H. R. "Bob" Haldeman *Watergate criminal*
THE HUMAN HAIRPIN   Harry "The Human Scissors" Harris *bantamweight champ 1901–02*
THE BARBER   Sal Maglie *"brushback" pitcher*
SHAVEY   Kenneth Lee *'40s locality mayor of NY's Chinatown*
WIG   Ralph Weigel *catcher*

Gimps

CRIPPLE   Clarence Lofton *blues pianist*
CRIP   Lou Polli *pitcher*
GIMPY   Lloyd Brown, Milt Pappas *pitchers*
OLD GIMPY   Robley D. Evans *U.S. admiral*
DEAF   Erasmus Smith *frontiersman, scout*
THE DEAF 'UN   James "Deaf" Burke *heavyweight champ 1833–39*
EARACHE   Bernhard "Benny" Meyer *outfielder 1913–15*
DUMMY   Luther Taylor *pitcher 1900–08*
VOICELESS   Tim O'Rourke *infielder 1890–95*

---

12. Beardless. Journalist Collins was suspected of sympathy with Castro of Cuba, whom she interviewed. Hence the witty sobriquet.
13. Baldy. If Mike Love's looks are anything to go by, the group should now be called the Beach Old Farts.

BLIND   Arthur Blake, Rev. Gary Davis, Lemon Jefferson, Willie Johnson, Willie McTell *bluesmen*
BLIND BOY FULLER   (Allen Fulton) *bluesman*
BLIND BOY GRUNT[14]   *pseudonym of Bob Dylan (Zimmerman)*
BLIND BOMBER   George Glanack *basketball scoring great*
BOGUS BLIND   Ben Covington *sighted blues singer*
ONE-EYED[15]   James Leo Connelly *gate crasher*
LOCKJAW   Eddie Davis *sax player*
SCARFACE   Al Capone *gangster*
ZIT   Carl F. Zittell *drama critic*
NO NOSE   Fred DeLucia *criminal*
NO-NECK   Walter Williams *outfielder*
HUMP   Bruce Campbell *outfielder*
CROOKBACK   Richard III *king of England, aka "Hog"*
ONE LUNG   George Smith *gambler*
ONE ARM   Hugh Daily *pitcher*
ONE-ARMED   Phil Kearny *Union general*
THREE FINGER   Mordecai "Miner" Brown *Hall of Famer pitcher*
THREE-FINGERED   William Jack White *criminal*
STUB   Leonard B. Allison *football coach* / James Smith *shortstop*
PEG LEG   Clayton Bates *one-legged tap dancer* / Joshua Howell *bluesman*
STUMPY   Floyd Brady *jazz trombonist*
BOWLEGS   Gene Miller *trombone, trumpet player*
THE BOWLEGGED ONE   Juan Fangio *car racer*
THE TOELESS WONDER   Ben "Automatic" Agajanian *football placekicker*
BLISTERFEET   Malcolm Hareen *ballet dancer*
BUNIONS   Rollie Zeider *Chicago infielder 1910–18*
WHIPLASH   Julio Navarro *pitcher*
TYPHOID MARY   Mary Mallon *cook, typhus source*
LUMBAGO   Archie Stimmell *Cincinnati pitcher 1901 (won 4, lost 14)*
THE BAYONNNE BLEEDER   Chuck Wepner *heavyweight contender*
THE FAINTING GENERAL   (see Franklin Pierce, U.S. Presidents)
WHEEZER   William Dell *Dodger pitcher 1915–17*
OLD ACHES AND PAINS   Luke Appling *baseball Hall of Famer*
STOOPING   Jack Gorman *infielder 1884*
BAD BODY   Thurman "Squatty" Munson *catcher*

14. Blind Boy Grunt. Other Dylan pseudonyms include "Tedham Porterhouse," "Bob Landy" (an anagram), and "Roosevelt Gook," a cute one now adopted by musician Al Kooper. The folk-rock bard sometimes checks into hotels under the name "Earl Grey."

15. One-Eyed. Connelly was a character of the '30s, a genius at bluffing his way free into sporting events. Ignominiously, he wound up as an usher at Chicago's Wrigley Field—which position he lost when he tried to evict Mr. Wrigley from a box seat, claiming the Cub's owner was a gate crasher. (Connelly's one good eye was green, by the way.)

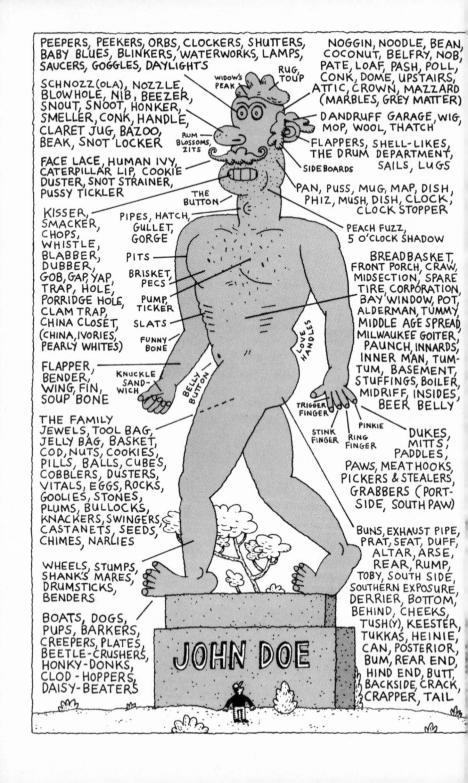

JOHN THOMAS

Apparatus

The bald-headed hermit, baloney, banjo, bone, business

Cock, crank

Dick, ding-a-ling, dingus, dink, dipstick, dong, dork, dummy

Equipment

Fern (to Steve Allen)

Gadget, giggle stick

Hickory stick, hose

Jack Robinson, jelly roll, johnson, John Thomas, joint, Jolly Roger

Little Elvis (to Elvis), love muscle

Meat (and two vegetables), middle leg, mutton dagger

Old man, one-eyed trouser snake, organ

Pecker, peter, pocket rocket, pole, pork sword, prick, privates, pud, putz

Rod

The salami, schlong, schmuck, schwanz, short arm, skin flute

Third leg, thrill hammer, tool, tube steak

The unemployed, unit

Wang, wazoo, weiner, wick, the wife's best friend, wire

Sometimes called: boner, hard on, stiffie, woodie

Temporary home of the Silver Bullet

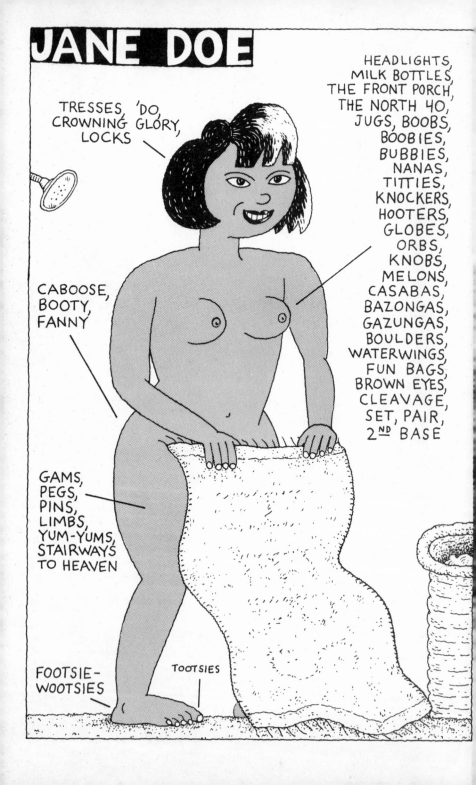

JANE DOE

TRESSES, 'DO,
CROWNING GLORY,
LOCKS

HEADLIGHTS,
MILK BOTTLES,
THE FRONT PORCH,
THE NORTH 40,
JUGS, BOOBS,
BOOBIES,
BUBBIES,
NANAS,
TITTIES,
KNOCKERS,
HOOTERS,
GLOBES,
ORBS,
KNOBS,
MELONS,
CASABAS,
BAZONGAS,
GAZUNGAS,
BOULDERS,
WATERWINGS,
FUN BAGS,
BROWN EYES,
CLEAVAGE,
SET, PAIR,
2ND BASE

CABOOSE,
BOOTY,
FANNY

GAMS,
PEGS,
PINS,
LIMBS,
YUM-YUMS,
STAIRWAYS
TO HEAVEN

FOOTSIE-
WOOTSIES

TOOTSIES

LADY JANE

Ace of spades, alley (Cupid's), aphrodisiacal tennis court

Base (3rd), beard, beaver, bunny, butterfly, business, box

Canyon, clam (bearded), cockpit, coffee house, cookie, cooze, crack, crumpet

Down there, dumb glutton

Et cetera, eye that weeps when most pleased

Fart daniel, fish pond, fumblers' hall, furburger, fuzz

Gash, gigi, golden donut, gravy maker, grotto (mossy), growler

Hair pie, happy valley, hog's eye, honey pot

Inglenook, it, itcher

Jack Nastyface, jampot, jelly roll

Keyhole, kitchen-kitty, kitten

Lady Jane, lamb-pit, lapland, lobsterpot, love canal, low countries

Manhole, melting pot, monkey, monosyllable, Mother of St. Patrick, mound, muff

Needlecase, nookie

Old hat, organ grinder, oven, oyster

Pen wiper, poontang, privates, pussy, Quiff, quim

Receiving set, ring-dang-do

Saddle, slit, slot, snapper, snatch, sportsmans' gap, sugar scoop

Tail, teazle, tickle-toby, tootsie-wootsie, twat

Uglies, under-dimple, upright wink

Vage, Venus (temple of), vertical smile

Where-uncle's-doodle-goes, wim-wam, works

"Y" (the), yoni, you-know-what, Zero

2
VIOLENCE ARE BLUE

Pen Names Department

CRIME & PUNISHMENT

Valero admitted on the stand that he was known as K.P. but insisted it stood for Kind Person. Several witnesses testified it meant King Pimp.

—News Item

PUBLIC ENEMY NO. 1   John Dillinger *bank robber, aka "Kill Crazy"*

PUBLIC ENEMY NO. 2   George "Baby Face" Nelson *murderer (alias Lester M. Gillis)*

HOMICIDE HANK   Henry "The Human Buzzsaw" Armstrong *welterweight champ 1938–40*

SUICIDE   Ted Elder *rodeo rider*

THE KILLER[1]   Jerry Lee Lewis *rock pianist, singer*

KILLER   Carl Banks *football lineman* / Joe Pirro *dance instructor* / Waldec Kowalski *pro wrestler*

STRANGLER   Ed Lewis *pro wrestler (when it was for real)*

THE BOSTON STRANGLER   Albert De Salvo *murderer*

ASSASSIN[2]   Jack Tatum *football linebacker*

HITMAN   Thomas "The Motor City Cobra" Hearns *middleweight champ 1981*

THE ENFORCER[3]   Frank Nitti *"Syndicate" killer* / Dave Schultz *hockey goon*

---

1. The Killer. Rock & roll original Jerry Lee ("Whole Lotta Shakin' Goin' On!") calls himself Killer, in public, often . . . either despite or because of his wives' and children's marked tendency to expire prematurely.

2. Assassin. A linebacker for the highly successful Oakland Raiders of the late '70s, Tatum's job was to clobber opposing pass-catchers. He managed to paralyze one for life. When he retired from the game, he wrote a book deploring violence in football.

3. The Enforcer. Schultz, aka "The Hammer," was employed by Fred "Fog" Sherro for the "Broadstreet Bullies," the highly successful Philadelphia Flyers of the mid-'70s. Schultz could neither skate nor shoot. His job was to punch out opposing players. After he retired, he wrote a book deploring violence in hockey.

THE CZAR OF THE UNDERWORLD   Arnold "Mr. Big" Rothstein
THE QUEEN OF CRIME   Agatha Christie *mystery writer*
KING OF THE MOONSHINERS   W. R. Gooch *distiller*
KING OF THE PIMPS   Charles "Lucky" Luciano *mobster*
THE MAYFLOWER MADAM, THE HAPPY HOOKER   (see Love & Sex)
THE FLIM FLAM MAN   Louis P. Mastriana *con artist*
THE GREAT IMPOSTOR   Stephen Weinberg *impersonator*
THE SPIDERMAN RAPIST   Tyrone Graham *NYC fire escape climber*
THE BOBBED HAIR BANDIT   Celia Cooney *Brooklyn bank robber*
THE KISSING BANDIT   Morganna Cottrell *sports enthusiast*
THE BABBLING BURGLAR   Richard C. Morrison *loquacious thief*
THE BASE BURGLER   Lou Brock *baseball speedster*
IFFY THE DOPESTER   Malcolm Bingay *bookie, oddsmaker*
SLEUTH   Tom Fleming *outfielder 1899–1902*
CRACKDOWN   U. S. Johnson *FDR cabinet member, aka "Iron Pants"*
THE SUBWAY VIGILANTE   Bernhard Goetz *shot 4 alleged muggers 1984*
SHERIFF   David Harris, Hal Lee *'30s outfielders*
CITATION   Lloyd Merriman *outfielder—named for the 1948 Triple Crown Winner*
JAILBIRD (JAYBIRD)   Burl Coleman *blues harmonica player*
THE BIRDMAN OF ALCATRAZ   Robert Franklin Stroud *eccentric inmate*
PENITENTIARY FACE   Jeffrey Leonard *outfielder*
GATES   William Brown *ex-con turned Tigers slugger 1963–75*
COLONEL WARDEN   *Winston Churchill's WWII code name*
MAXIMUM   John Sirica *U.S. federal judge*
JUDGE LOUIS[4]   Louis "Lepke" Buchalter *Murder Inc., capo*
THE CAPITAL PUNISHER   Frank "Hondo" Howard *Washington Senators slugger*
THE HANGMAN OF EUROPE   Reinhard Heydrich *Nazi SS deputy director*
THE BUFFALO HANGMAN[5]   Grover Cleveland *22nd and 24th U.S. prexy*
THE LORD HIGH EXECUTIONER   Albert Anastasia *hitman, aka "The Mad Hatter"*
HANGING JUDGE   Roy Bean *"The Only Law West of the Pecos"* / Isaac Parker, Sir Francis Page, and John Toler, Earl of Norbury *British magistrates*
THE HOODLUM PRIEST   Fr. Charles Clarke *prison chaplain*
TURN 'EM LOOSE BRUCE[6]   Bruce Wright *lenient NYC magistrate*

---

4. Judge Louis. Dubbed "Lepkeleh" by his doting mom (it means "Little Louis") and "Judge" by the competing mobsters he sentenced to death. Wound up in the Sing Sing hot seat, 1944.

5. Buffalo Hangman. While Sheriff of Buffalo, NY, Cleveland dealt with a law-enforcement officers' strike by personally pulling the rope on a convicted murderer.

6. Turn 'Em Loose Bruce. Judge Wright has been known to dash off the odd antifeminist verse under the names "Nabru Nolef" and "Enog Sinep." (Read 'em backward to get the joke.)

Big Shots Department

WEAPONS

PISTOL   Richard Allen *Motown drummer* / Pete Maravich *basketball Hall of Fame forward*

TWO GUN[1]   Leland Verain "The Cowboy" Alterie *Chicago gangster* / Morris A. Cohen *Chinese folk hero* / Bill Hart *Dodger 3rd baseman*

SHOTGUN   Robert Johnson *blues musician* / George Shuba *Dodger outfielder*

MACHINE GUN[2]   George R. Kelly *bank robber*

MACHINE GUN JACK McGURRIN   (Vincent Gebardi) *hitman*

MACHINE GUN MOLLY   Monica Smith *bank robber*

THE RIFLE   Sam Etchevary *quarterback*

THE KENTUCKY RIFLE   Glen Combs *basketball forward*

THE READING RIFLE   Carl "Skoonj" Furillo *Dodger outfielder*

THE SPRINGFIELD RIFLE   Vic Raschi *Yankee pitcher*

AUTOMATIC   Ben Agajanian *football placekicker, aka "The Toeless Wonder"*

TRIGGER   Herman Alpert *jazz musician* / Mike Coppola *mobster*

SHOOTY   Mack Babbit *2nd baseman*

KID SHOTS   Louis Madison *trumpeter*

CROSSFIRE   Earl Alonzo Moore *erratic fastball pitcher 1901–14*

VOLLEY   Voltaire DeFault *jazz violinist*

BULLET   Bill Dudley *football speedster* / Bob Feller *Cleveland Indians pitching ace, aka "Rapid Robert"*

BUCKSHOT   Thomas Brown *basketball forward* / Glen Wright *shortstop*

DUM DUM   Jose Luis Pacheco *fighter*

SLUG   Harry Heilmann *Hall of Fame Detroit outfielder 1914–32*

BEBE   Charles Gregory Rebozo *Nixon's friend* (see also "The Aerosol King," Assumed Titles)

DUD   Wilbur Bascomb *jazz trumpeter*

TANK   Mike Williams *heavyweight* / Paul Younger *fullback*

MINI TANK   Leroy Hughes *football back*

HOWITZER HAYNES   Leroy "The Sable Sniper" Haynes *fighter*

THE MEXICAN SPITFIRE[3]   Lupe Velez *movie actress*

BATTLESHIP   Albert Leduc *hockey defenseman*

GUNBOAT SMITH   Edward J. Smyth *ring referee*

---

1. Two Gun. Morris Cohen was a nice Canadian Jewish boy who traveled to and through China as the personal bodyguard of "The Last Warlord," Sun Yat-sen. Really.

2. Machine Gun Kelly is supposed, in the process of surrendering to the F.B.I., to have coined the term "G-men." Hoover said so, right in the *Reader's Digest*. Must be true.

3. The Mexican Spitfire. Lupe Velez's name is inextricably intertwined with that of John "Duke" Wayne in Hollywood scandal lore. The names of the rest of the football team are long forgotten.

SUB[4]   Carl Mays *pitcher*
BAZOOKA[5]   Bob Burns *vaudevillian* / Raphael Limon *lightweight*
THE FLAME THROWER   Harry Fanok *Cards pitcher 1963–64*
THE TOY CANNON   Jimmy Wynn *strong-armed Astros outfielder*
BOOM BOOM CANNON   (Freddie Picarilleo) *rock singer*
CANNONBALL   Julian Adderley *jazz sax master* / Eddie Martin *bantamweight champ 1924–25*
TORPEDO BILLY   Thomas W. Murphy *fighter*
TOM THE BOMB   Tom Tracey *Canadian football running back*
THE BLOND BOMBSHELL   Jean Harlow (Harlean Carpenter) *screen sex goddess, aka "The Platinum Blond"*
THE BRAZILIAN BOMBSHELL   Carmen Miranda *singer, dancer*
THE TIDAL BASIN BOMBSHELL   (see "Argentine Firecracker," below)
DYNAMITE   Joey Brooks *saloon keeper, arsonist* / Seraphim Post, Gus Sonnenberg *football stars*
KID DYNAMITE   Jorge Morales *fighter*
LITTLE MISS DYNAMITE   Brenda Lee *pop & country singer*
MR. DYNAMITE   (see Misters)
THE ARGENTINE FIRECRACKER[6]   Fanne Foxe *stripper*
POISON   David Kotey *featherweight champ 1975*
OLD POISON   Nels Stewart *hockey scoring great*
BIG POISON   Paul Waner *Pirates slugger, Hall of Fame*
LITTLE POISON   Lloyd Waner *brother of the above, ditto*
THE WHIP   Ewell Blackwell *Cincinnati sidearm pitcher*
BUGGY WHIP   Gary Maddox *Phillies outfield ace, aka "The Secretary of Defense"*
SPIKE   Lindley Armstrong Jones[7]   *comic-musician* / Terrence Allen Milligan *British comic genius and "Goon"*
BIG SPIKE   (see "Stormin' Gorman," Weather)
CAP THE KNIFE   Caspar Weinberger *Reagan's secretary of defense*

4. Sub. Sidearm (submarine-ball) pitcher Mays pitched 3,000 innings and won 208 games over a fifteen-year span. In 1920, as a Yankee, he beaned Ray Chapman, Cleveland shortstop, and killed him. Such a thing has never happened before or since.

5. Bazooka. Burns's act was to tell jokes while assembling a series of metal tubes into a musical instrument he called a "Bazooka," which he threatened to play. WWII G.I.s named their antitank weapon after his prop. The bubblegum people named their product after the gun. So it goes.

6. The Argentine Firecracker. While plying her trade in the nation's capital, Ms. Foxe wound up in a fountain disporting with hitherto-conservative congressman from Arkansas Wilbur Mills for the benefit of policemen and news photographers; hence "The Tidal Basin Bombshell." She was born Annabel Batistella. Mills was aka "Mr. Taxes."

7. Spike Jones. Son of a Union Pacific Railroad worker, Jones picked up his nickname naturally enough. His son Spike Jr. inherited the corny sound-effects band and nickname. *Los Angeles Examiner* columnist Bill Kennedy tried calling him "Tack," but it didn't stick. Spike Jr.'s son's name is Taylor. Says Spike, "The Spike stops here."

Rank and Serial Number Department

THE MILITARY

GENERAL   Alvin Crowder *American League workhorse pitcher 1926–36*
GENERAL MUM   (see William "Tippecanoe" Harrison, U.S. Presidents)
GENERAL TOM THUMB   Charles S. Straton *circus performer*
THE TOASTMASTER GENERAL   Georgie Jessel *comedian*
ADMIRAL   Claude Berry *catcher*
ADMIRAL Q   Franklin Roosevelt *WWII code name*
COLONEL WARDEN   Winston Churchill *WWII code name*
THE KENTUCKY COLONEL   Earle Combs *Yankee outfielder 1924–32, Hall of Famer, aka "The Mail Carrier"*
THE LITTLE COLONEL   Harold "Pee Wee" Reese *Dodger shortstop 1940–58*
COMMANDER CINQUE   (Donald deFreeze) *leader of the Symbionese Liberation Army, abductor of Patty "Tania" Hearst*
COMMANDER CODY   George Frayne *country rock musician*
COMMANDER ZERO   Eden Pastora Gomez *"Contra" leader*
MAJOR   Edward Bowes *radio talent-show host* / George Magerkurth *umpire*
THE MAJOR   Ralph Houk *managed Yanks, Tigers, Bosox*
CAPTAIN   Daryl Dragon *pianist*
CAPTAIN BEEFHEART   (Don Van Vliet) *rock musician*
CAPTAIN HOOK   George "Sparky" Anderson *Reds, Tigers manager*
CAPTAIN MIDNIGHT   John MacDougal *"pirate" broadcaster*
CAPTAIN OUTRAGEOUS   Ted Turner *financier, aka "The Capsize Kid"*
CAPTAIN SHRIMP   Myles Standish *colonist*
SARGE   James Bagby, George Connally, Gary Matthews, etc. *ballplayers*
OLD SARGE   Hoyt Wilhelm *all-time leader games pitched, relief wins*
CORPORAL   Izzy Schwartz *flyweight champ 1927*
CORPORAL VIOLET,[1] THE LITTLE CORPORAL   Napoleon "Little Boney" Bonaparte
LITTLE NAPOLEON   John "Muggsy" McGraw *Giants manager 1902–32*
THE GLADIATOR   Louis Rogers "Pete" Browning *outfielder 1882–94*
WARRIOR   Fumika Hanada *fighter*
THE WILDCAT WARRIOR   (see "Brown Bomber," Assorted Mayhem)
THE HAPPY WARRIOR[2]   Alfred Emanuel "Al" Smith *politician*
BATTLE HAWK   Kujoshi Kazama *fighter*
THE MARINE   George LaBlanche (George Blais) *middleweight champ 1889*

1. Corporal Violet. During Napoleon's first exile, his loyalists in France would cautiously ask citizens, "Do you like violets?"—that is, "Do you want him back?"
2. The Happy Warrior. Hubert "Pinky" "The Hump" Humphrey, like Smith a liberal democrat, adopted this sobriquet, and its military connotations perhaps caused Jimmy Carter to eulogize Humphrey as "Hubert Horatio Hornblower."

THE FIGHTING MARINE   James Joseph "Gene" Tunney *heavyweight champ 1926–28*
BIG-NAVY CLAUDE   Claude A. Swanson, *FDR's secretary of the navy*
SAILOR   Jack Sharkey *heavyweight champ 1932, aka "The Boston Gob"*
THE SAILOR'S FRIEND   Samuel Plimsoll *British shipping reformer*
SOLDIER BOY   George Curry *pitcher*
COMMANDO KELLY   Charles Kelly *American WWII hero*
BOMBARDIER   Billy Wells *European heavyweight champ 1911*
GUNNER   James Moir *European heavyweight champ 1906–09*
TAILGUNNER JOE [3]   Joseph McCarthy *senator from Wisconsin*
ARNIE'S ARMY   *fans of golfer Arnold Palmer*
BUNKER   Carmen Hill *National League pitcher 1915–30, aka "Specs"*
TAPS   John Gallagher *basketball star*
HALF-MAST MEL   Melvin Thompson *congressman*
ANGEL OF THE BATTLEFIELDS   Clara Barton *Red Cross founder*
ANTI-WAR KNUTSON   Harold Knutson *isolationist politician*
FATHER OF PEACE   Andrea Doria *Italian admiral, statesman*

Sticks and Stones Department

ASSORTED MAYHEM

MR. ATTACK   Maxwell Taylor *U.S. general, WWII & Korea*
ATTACK   Takeo Harada *bantamweight*
THE MANASSA MAULER   William Harrison "Jack" Dempsey *heavyweight champ 1919–26, aka "Jack the Giant Killer"*
THE YORKSHIRE RIPPER   Peter Suthcliffe *mass murderer*
THE TIPTON SLASHER   William Perry *bareknuckle champ 1850*
VLAD THE IMPALER [1]   Vlad Teppes *the original Dracula 1432–77*
THE MAD BOMBER   Daryl Lamonica *quarterback*
THE BRONX BOMBER   Alex Ramos *fighter*
THE BROWN BOMBER, THE BROWN BLUDGEON, THE BROWN EMBALMER, THE LICORICE LASHER   Joe Louis (Barrow) *heavyweight champ 1937–49, aka "The Brown Behemoth," "The Tan Thunderbolt," "Black Beauty," "Sable Sphinx," "Ring Robot," "Wildcat Warrior," "Alabam' Assassin, " etc. . . .*

3. Tailgunner Joe. Before setting out on a witch hunt for commies, McCarthy had a distinguished military career, and still holds the record for rounds of ammo fired when not in combat. He liked mowing down palm trees.

1. Vlad the Impaler. A Transylvanian noble and recently reinstated folk hero in the Soviet Union, Vlad opposed the Turkish domination of his homeland by sitting Turks down hard on sharpened sticks. Did it to thousands of 'em.

BLIND BOMBER   George Glanack *basketball*
BOMBER   Mark Bomback 1980 *Met pitcher* / Sir Arthur T. "Ginger" Harris *British Air Marshall WWII* / Maurice Van Robays *Pirate outfielder 1939–46*
THE BROWN BLASTER   George Sisler *aka "Gorgeous George," St. Louis Browns 1st baseman 1915–29, Hall of Famer*
BRUISER   Frank Kinard *football Hall of Famer*
THE ATOMIC PUNCHER   Rocky Graziano (Thomas Rocco Barbella) *middleweight champ 1947–48*
THE BROCKTON BLOCKBUSTER   Rocky Marciano (Rocco Marchegiano) *heavyweight champ 1952–56*
THE SMASHER[2]   Carry Nation *anti-saloon activist*
SMASHER   Robert Asher *football player*
SLASHER   Ted Atkinson *British jockey*
RIPPER   Jimmy Collins *1st baseman 1931–41*
WHIPPER   Billy Watson *Canadian wrestling champ*
SLUGGER   Jack Burns *replaced Sisler (see above)*
SOCKER   Charles F. Coe *respected publisher*
BREAKER[3]   Harry Morant *Australian soldier*
BONECRUSHER   Joseph Bernstein *wrestler* / James Smith *heavyweight champ*
SCRAPPER   Francis Blackwell *blues guitarist*
BATTLING   Christopher Battalino *featherweight champ 1929–32* / Bob LaFollette *Wisconsin populist leader 1855–1925* / Siki (Louis Phal) *light heavyweight champ 1923*
BATTLING LEVINSKY[4]   (Barney Lebrowitz) *light heavyweight champ 1916–20*
BATTLING NELSON   (Oscar Neilson) *lightweight champ 1908–10, aka "The Durable Dane"*
FIGHTING   Masahiko Harada *featherweight champ 1962–63, bantamweight champ 1965–68* / Joe Hooker *Union general*
FIGHTING GUY   Guy V. Henry *colonel, WWII*
THE FIGHTING FOOL   (see "Jack Sharkey," Reptiles, Amphibians & Fish)
THE FIGHTING PARSON   William G. Brownlow *politician*
THE PULVERIZING POLE   Jadwiga Jedryejowska *tennis player*
SLAMMIN' SAMMY   Sam Snead *golf champ, aka "The West Virginia Hillbilly"*
JOLTIN' JOE   Joseph DiMaggio *aka "The Yankee Clipper"*
LARRUPIN' LOU   Lou Gehrig (see "The Durable Dutchman," Them)
SWEET SWINGIN'   Billy Williams *sluggin' Cubbies outfielder 1959–75*

2. The Smasher. Carry Nation called her attacks on bar rooms "Hatchetation."
3. Breaker. The recent film was based upon an actual Boer war event. Morant got his nickname from his way with wild horses, recalling another war hero, Hector of Troy, aka "The Tamer of Horses."
4. Battling Levinsky. A character in an age of characters, he trained under the supervision of his equally wacky sister, Leaping Lena. Among his other tags were "King," "The Furious Fishmonger," and "The Mad Mackerel Merchant."

SLAPSIE MAXIE   Maxey Rosenbloom *light heavyweight champ 1930–34*
SPANKY   George Emmett Phillips McFarland *actor (Our Gang)* / Elaine McFarlane *singer (Our Gang)*
KNOCKY   John Parker *pianist*
CRUNCHY   Bill Cronin *Bosox catcher 1928–31*
SCRATCHLEY   George Brown *aviator*
SCRATCH   Lee Perry *musician*
KICK   John "Father" Kelly *catcher 1882–84*
RIP   Arthur Basset *banjo player* / Elmore Torn *actor*
HACK   Lewis Wilson *Dodger, Cub outfielder 1923–34, Hall of Famer*
PUNCH   (see Drink)
YANK   John Lawson (Lausen) *jazz trumpet player*
TUG   Francis McGraw *Mets and Phillies ace reliever 1965–84*
SLAM   Leroy Stewart *jazz bass player*
BAM   Brian McCall   *Palehose hopeful 1962–63*
BIFF   William J. McGuire *actor, playwright*
SMACK   Fletcher Henderson *jazz pianist, arranger*
SQUASH   Frank Wilson *outfielder 1924–28*
BASH   Albert "Pete" Compton *outfielder 1911–18*
KAYO   John Dottley *football player*
NEWK   John Newcombe *Australian tennis champ, sportswriter*
STUFF   Hezekiah Smith *jazz musician*
HIT AND MUSS   Hitler and Mussolini *(to Allied servicemen)*
TAP   Art Harris *fighter*
BUMP   Irving Hadley *pitcher 1926–41 (walked 1,442 batters)* / Elliott Taylor Wills *Texas Rangers 2nd baseman 1977–82, son of Hall of Famer Maury Wills*
BUMPS   Hubert Myers *jazz sax player*
PLOW 'EM UNDER   Henry A. Wallace *FDR's secretary of agriculture*
ROUGHHOUSE   Harold Ross *editor of* The New Yorker
JOHNNY BLOOD   John McNally *running back 1925–39, Hall of Famer*
GYP THE BLOOD   Harry Horowitz *NYC criminal circa 1912, electrocuted*
GUTS   Ishimatsu Suzuki *lightweight champ 1974–76*
OLD BLOOD AND GUTS   General George S. Patton
BLOODY MARY   Mary Tudor *Queen of England*
THE BAYONNE BLEEDER[5]   Chuck Wepner *heavyweight contender*
THE GRIM REAPER   David Stockman *Reaganomicist*
DEATH   Stephen Oliver *fighter*
DEATH'S HEAD   Hermann von Hoth *Nazi general*
THE ANGEL OF DEATH   Josef Mengele *war criminal*
KISS OF DEATH   Evelyn Mittleman *gun moll*

---

5. The Bayonne Bleeder. The endless series of "Rocky" movies is based on the character of this hemophiliac pugilist, a game opponent for Ali, Holmes, et al., and also white.

DEATH TO FLYING THINGS   Bob Ferguson *baseball manager, infielder 1871–94*
TOMBSTONE   Richard Jackson *defensive end*
HOLLY WOODLAWN   (Harold Ajezenberg) *Warhol superstar*
PAINLESS PARKER   (Edgar Rudolph Randolph) *dentist*

This Is My Rifle and This Is My Gun Department

ARMAMENTS

The army issued them as USMK2 fragmentation grenades, but the men who tossed them called them "pineapples." The airforce designated it the F-106 fighter-bomber and provided it with a sexy title, Thunderchief, but the men who flew it called it "Thud" and "The Lead Sled." To their crews, the Sherman M-4 tanks of World War II were "Ronsons" (because "they light up every time"). In their amphibious mode, Shermans had "D.D." (for Duplex Drive) prominently inscribed. To the tank corps that stood for Donald Duck.

The Vietnam-era CH 47 helicopter was officially a Chinook, pronounced by all grunts "Shithook." The H2-1 was, on sight, a "Flying Banana," the HH-53 a "Jolly Green Giant," the UH-1 "Hog" and UG-1 "Huey." The C-47 helicopter gunship was to one and all (and to Peter, Paul, and Mary's great distress) "Puff the Magic Dragon."

The army tradition may be to call a spade an entrenching device, but there's also an old enlisted man's tradition to call 'em like you sees 'em.

So, in the Civil War, the Union battery gun was obviously a "Coffee Mill." The World War I Colt field machine gun was plainly a "Potato Digger," and the lightly armed World War II P-26A fighter plane a "Peashooter."

Enemy armaments are known only by shape, sound, and nickname. A World War I German siege gun was, to the ear at least, a "Farting Fannie," and a German hand grenade was, by sight, a "Potato Masher." The World War II Schmeisser was, by the sound of it, a "Burp Gun," the same way a Nebelwerfer 150-mm rocket was a "Screaming Meemie" and a V-I a "Buzz Bomb." By sight, the Luftwaffe's mighty F-6F was a "Pregnant Bathtub."

Today, we have satellites and spies to photograph the enemy's arsenal. But the stuff still needs nicknaming, and somebody is doing a great job.

When the Soviet Antonov An-2 fighter was unveiled, he dubbed it "Colt." Model An-11 he called "Coot." He was on a creative roll. An-12 was "Cub." It is the army way to maintain traditions, but change with the times. The recent An-22 was labeled "Cock" . . . and the latest Soviet airborne threat to our way of life is officially nicknamed "Coke."

Speaking in General Terms Department

OFFICERS

Like soldiers everywhere, U.S. troops have awarded nicknames to their officers. Some of them are even printable. Revolutionary war leaders included "Mad" Anthony Wayne, "Lighthorse" Harry Lee, and Ethan Allen, "The Green Mountain Boy" and self-styled "King of Vermont." "Old Hickory" Andy Jackson and "Granny" Henry Dearborn commanded in the War of 1812, out of which arose two unique nicknames—"Old Ironsides" for the U.S.S. *Constitution,* and "Uncle Sam," the mocking tag applied to one Sam Wilson of Troy, New York, an army meat inspector who never failed to stamp his initials, U.S., on barrels of salt meat, however lousy.

The War Between the States (sometimes nicknamed "The Civil War") featured generals Thomas "Stonewall" Jackson and Ulysses S. "Hug" Grant. Jackson was sometimes "Fool Tom" and "Blue Light Elder." Behind *his* back, Grant was "Unconditional Surrender" and "Butcher."

Robert E. Lee was "Old Ace of Spades," and James Ewell Brown Stuart both "JEB" and "Beauty." George T. Anderson was "Old Tige," Winfield Scott "Old Fuss and Feathers," Joseph Hooker "Fighting Joe," and William Tecumseh Sherman both "Yes Ma'am" and "Mad Tom." "Little Phil" Sheridan was short, "One-Armed Phil" Kearney had indeed lost an arm, but William F. "Baldy" Smith had a full head of hair.

Benjamin "The Beast" Butler was unpopular, even for a general. He was called "Spoons," because it was alleged he stole cutlery.

During the Great War, or War of the Nations, the first to be honored with the nickname "World War," American troops were commanded by John Joseph "Black Jack" Pershing. "Black Jack" was a public-relations euphemism for the title Pershing had earned commanding Negro troops in the 10th Cavalry. Eddie Rickenbacker, fighter pilot, received the honorific "Ace of Aces," and Eugene Bullard, the first black combat aviator, flew with the Lafayette Escadrille, earning both the Croix de Guerre and the title "Black Swallow of Death."

Admirals of World War II include William F. "Bull" Halsey, "Eagle-Eye Ernie" King, Husband E. "Hubby" Kimmel, and Robley D. "Gimpy" Evans. Among the generals: Holland "Howlin' Mad" Smith, Henry "Hap" Arnold, aka "Do-It-Yesterday," Carl "Tooey" Spaatz, "Dug-out Doug" MacArthur, and "The Old Man," George Patton, aka "Green Hornet," "Flash Gordon," "Two Gun," and "Old Blood and Guts." ("Sure," says the apocryphal G.I. "His guts, and our blood.")

Family Names Department

THE MOB

In 1986, reputed members of the Genovese La Cosa Nostra family went on trial in Springfield, Massachusetts, but legal proceedings soon broke down. At issue was the question of whether revealing the defendants' nicknames would "obviate jury confusion" as the prosecution argued, or "have a prejudicial effect on the jury" as the defense maintained.

You be the judge. Alleged "capo" of the New England Mafia is Francesco Scibelli, seventy-two. Witnesses and wiretaps refer to Mr. Scibelli as "Skyball," "Skiball," "Sky," "Ski," and "Frankie." His co-defendants include Albert "Baba" Scibelli, and Ricardo "Soggy" Songini. Pretty tame stuff, huh?

Back in the '30s, when the G-men nabbed Abe "Kid Twist" Reles and made a canary out of him, they netted a mob of much more spectacular monikers: the *noms de guerre* of Murder Incorporated's officers and soldiers—"czars" and "hitmen."

Kid Twist related that the Syndicate bosses—Charles "Lucky" Luciano, Vito "Don Vitone" Genovese, Louis "Lepke" Buchalter, and Abner "Longy" Zwillman—had formed their own law-enforcement squad, placing its leadership in the capable hands of capos Benny "Bugsy" Siegel and Meyer "The Bug" Lansky. Kid Twist described to the cops in glowing detail the 500 contract hits of "Pittsburgh Phil" (Harry Strauss), as well as the work with blade, torch, bat, and gat performed by Vito "Socko" Gurino, Joe "Adonis" Doto, "Pretty" Levine, "Buggsy" Goldstein, "Dandy" Phil Kastel, "Gangy" Cohen, "Dasher" Abadano, "Dukey" Maffetore, "Happy" Maione, Jacob "Gurrah" Shapiro, and the immortal "Blue Jaw" Magoon.

Kid Twist's testimony was abruptly interrupted when he stepped out a high window while in round-the-clock protective custody.

But the organized crime bosses had learned their lesson. They became discreet, and put "The Mad Hatter," Albert "The Lord High Executioner" Anastasia, in complete control of Murder Inc.'s marketing, production, and quality control. Then "hit" *him.*

Yet there is good news on the underworld nickname front. We may never again see the likes of Alvin "Old Creepy" Karpis, Frank "The Enforcer" Nitti, Joe "Batty" Accardo, "Trigger" Burke or Mike "de Pike" Heitler . . . but the Manhattan U.S. attorney's office has these members of a Chinatown youth gang "The Ghost Shadows," under surveillance: Bing Far "Mongo" Yuen, Chiu Ping "Applehead" Wu, Jackie "Lobsterhead" Mool, David "Stinky Bug" Wong, and Steven "Itchy Ass" Yau.

3
HOUSEHOLD NAMES

Relatively Speaking Department

THE FAMILY

Who called the English teacher "Daddy-O"?

—Leiber and Stoller

FAMILY MAN   Aston Barrett *reggae musician (Wailer)*
MOTHER   Maybelle Carter *singer* / Walter Watson *baseball pitcher*
MOTHER JONES   (Mary Harris) *radical organizer*
MOMS MABLEY   (Loretta Mary Aiken) *comedian*
MA   Kate Barker *criminal matriarch, aka "Arizona Donnie Clark"* / Miriam Ferguson *Texas governor*
MA RAINEY   (Gertrude Malissa Pridgett) *singer, aka "Mother of the Blues"*
MAMA CASS ELLIOT   (Ellen Cohen) *singer (The Mamas and the Papas)*
MAMA LU   Louise Parks *dance troupe leader*
BIG MAMA   Willie Mae Thornton *blues singer*
LAST OF THE RED HOT MAMAS   Sophie Tucker (Sophia Kalish) *singer*
FATHER   John "Kick" Kelly *catcher*
FATHA   Earl Hines *jazz pianist*
DAD   Theodore Roberts *actor*
DADDY BIG BUCKS   (see "Phantom Angel," Religion & Mystery)
BIG DADDY   Don "Swamp Rat" Garlitz *car racer* / Gene Lipscomb *football player (OD'd)* / Ed Roth *cartoonist*
OLD DADDY   William V. S. Tubman *Liberian president*
DADDY OF THE BABY, FATHER OF THE HOMESTEAD   (see "The Drunken Tailor" Andy Johnson, U.S. Presidents)
PAPA BEAR   George Halas *father of the Chicago Bears*
PAPA DOC   François Duvalier *dictator, father of deposed dictator "Baby Doc"*
PAPA MUTT   Thomas Carey *trumpet player*

COOL PAPA[1]   James Bell *baseball Hall of Famer*

FUNNY PAPA   John T. Smith *singer*

PAPA   John Creech *fiddler* / Ernest Hemingway *writer* / Charlie Jackson *banjo player* / Jonathan "Jo" Jones *drummer* / Karl Marx *communist* / John Phillips *singer (The Mamas and the Papas)*

PAPPY   Greg Boyington *USAF major*

POP   John Corkhill, Jesse Haines, Charles Smith, Edward "Dimples" Tate, Wilver "Willie" Stargell *baseball players* / George Foster *tuba player* / Glenn Warner[2] *football coach*

POPS   Armstrong (see "Satchmo," Mouth) / John Henry Lloyd *baseball player* / Paul Whiteman *"The King of Jazz"*

MR. POPS   Arthur Fiedler *conductor (The Boston Pops)*

THE OLD MAN   (see "Old Blood and Guts," Assorted Mayhem)

DADA   Idi Amin *exiled Ugandan dictator*

BAPU   Mohandas K. Gandhi *Mahatma*

THE GODFATHER OF SOUL, SOUL BROTHER NO. 1 (see "Mr. Dynamite," Misters)

(STEP)FATHER OF HIS COUNTRY (see Washington, U.S. Presidents)

GRANDPA   Louis Jones *"Hee Haw" star*

FOXY GRANDPA   Jimmy Bannon *baseball player, brother of "Uncle Tom" Bannon, baseball player*

GRANDMA MOSES   Anna Mary (Robertson) Moses *painter*

GRANNY   Rutherford B. Hayes (see U.S. Presidents) / Grantland Rice *sportswriter*

OLD GRANNY   (see William "Tippecanoe" Harrison, U.S. Presidents)

AUNT JEMIMA   Edith Wilson *singer, actress (b. 1906)*

AUNT MOLLY JACKSON   (Mary Magdalan Garland) *C&W performer*

AUNTIE SAM   Anne Armstrong *U.S. ambassador*

UNCLE CORNPONE, BIG DADDY   (see "Landslide" Lyndon, U.S. Presidents)

UNCLE JUMBO   (see Grover "The Buffalo Hangman" Cleveland, U.S. Presidents)

UNCLE SAM   (see "Butcher" Ulysses S. Grant, U.S. Presidents)

UNCLE REMUS   Joel Chandler Harris *author*

UNCLE   Joe Cannon *Speaker of the House* / Walter Cronkite *anchorman* / Carl Laemmle *film producer* / Dave Macon *country musician*

UNCLE FLOYD   Floyd Vivino *comedian*

UNCLE MILTIE   Milton Berle (Berlinger) *comedian, aka "Mr. Television"*

UNCLE ROBBIE   Wilbert Robinson *baseball Hall of Fame player, manager*

COUSIN BRUCIE   Bruce Morrow *deejay*

COUSIN CHEAP   Hugh Carter, Jr. *cousin to Jimmy Carter*

COUSIN ED   Edward Barrow *baseball manager*

BROTHER CORNBREAD   (Joe Thomas) *jazz musician*

1. Cool Papa. Slugging outfielder and manager in the Negro Leagues, Bell was sometimes called "The Black Ty Cobb"—whatever that means.

2. Pop. Little League football is named "Pop Warner football" in honor of this particular father figure.

BASHFUL BROTHER OSWALD   (Beecher "Pete" Kirby) *dobro player*
LITTLE BROTHER   Eurreal Montgomery *blues pianist*
SISTER AMY   Amy Archer-Gillian *nurse, murderess*
SIS   John Winston Hopkins *baseball player*
TWIN   Mike Sullivan *fighter*
SON BRIMMER   (Will Shade) *bluesman*
SON   Eddie James House *bluesman* / Jim Seals *Chicago bluesman*
SON OF SAM   David Berkowitz *murderer*
SONNY   Ralph Barger *Hell's Angel* / Salvatore Bono *singer* / Liston (see "The Big Ugly Bear," Mammals) / Theodore Rollins *sax player* / Edward Stitt *sax player* / Bowen Charleston Tufts *actor*
SONNY TERRY   (Teddell Saunders) *harmonica player, singer*
JUNIOR   James W. Gilliam *Dodger great* / Robert G. Johnson[3] *stock car racer* / Julian Mance *pianist* / etc.
JUNIOR WELLS   (Amos Blackmore) *bluesman*
LITTLE JUNIOR   Herman Parker *singer*
GUITAR JUNIOR   Luther Johnson, Jr. *guitarist*
BOBO[4] JUNIOR   Bobby Bonds *baseball player*

Just Don't Call Me Late for Dinner Department

FOOD

HUNGRY   Joe Lewis *bunko'd Oscar Wilde on 17th St., 1882*
ERIC STARVE GALT   *alias of James Earl "The Mole" Ray*

Appetizers

PRETZELS   John Pezzullo *pitcher*
CHIPS RAFFERTY   (John Goffage) *Australian actor*
POPCORN   Kirby Walters *rodeo performer*
PEANUTS   Herbert Holland, Michael Hucko *musicians* / Harry Lowrey *outfielder*
GOOBER   William Zuber *pitcher*
THE CHESTNUT   Edwin Austin Abbey *writer*
NACHO   Ignacio Jiminez *fighter*
CHEESE   Al Schweitzer *outfielder*
COLBY JACK   John Coombs *pitcher, manager*
CRACKERS[1]   Sylvester Graham *health food pioneer*

3. Junior. According to Tom Wolfe, "Junior Johnson is the Great American Hero, yes!"

4. Bobo Junior. According to the "Talking Baseball" song, "Bobby Bonds could play for everyone." As indeed he did, and ranks 5th on the all-time strikeout list.

1. Crackers. The well-known biscuit was invented by Sylvester, whose diet and exercise regimen was espoused by health-conscious celebrities such as Amelia Bloomer.

CRACKER   Ray Schalk *Hall of Fame catcher*
SOUP   Clarence Campbell *baseball player*
SOUPY SALES   (Milton Hines) *comedian*
PEA SOUP   George Dumont *pitcher*
DINTY MOORE   James H. Moore *restaurateur*
NOODLES ZUPO   Frank Zupo *catcher*
CHILI   Charles Davis *outfielder*

Meat

MEAT   Jim Brosnan *pitcher 1954–63, aka "Professor"*
RAW MEAT   Bill Rodgers *2nd baseman 1915*
MEAT LOAF   (Marvin Lee Aday) *pop singer*
BEEF   Arthur Wheeler *football player*
BIG BEEFHEAD   (see Grover "The Buffalo Hangman" Cleveland, U.S. Presidents)
CAPTAIN BEEFHEART   (Don Van Vliet) *musician, composer*
T-BONE   Aaron Walker *guitarist*
HAMBONE   Willie Newbern *blues guitarist*
HAM   Leonard Davis *jazz trumpeter* / Robert Hamilton Hyatt *1st baseman*
PORK CHOP   John Hoffman *catcher* / Jerome Smith *jazz musician*
PIGMEAT[2]   Dewey Alamo "Judge" Markham *comedian*
MUTTONLEG   Ted Donnelly *trombonist*
LIVER   Walter "Gee" Ancker *pitcher 1915*
A. VENISON   Ezra Pound (pseudonym)
BARBECUE BOB   (Robert Hicks) *blues guitarist*
DOUBLE CHEESEBURGER   Reggie Cleveland *rotund pitcher 1969–82, aka "Snacks"*
THE HAMBURGER KING   Doug Broome *restaurateur*

Vegetables

POTATO   Carlos Valdez *jazz musician*
HOT POTATO   Luke Hamlin *Dodger stalwart pitcher*
THE BIG POTATO   William E. "The Idaho Lion" Borah *isolationist Idaho senator* / Carlos Pascual *pitcher 1950*
LITTLE POTATO   Camilo Pascual *pitcher 1954–71 (little brother of "Big Potato")*
THE AROOSTOOK POTATO   Ralph Owen Brewster *Maine senator*
POTATOES   Julius Kauffman *mobster*
SPUD[3]   Spurgeon Chandler *baseball commissioner* / Lyle Murphy *sax player*
WAVY GRAVY   (Hugh Romney) *hippie prankster*

2. Pigmeat. In his vaudeville act, it was Markham who was introduced with the immortal phrase "Here come de judge!"

3. Spud. "Spud" Webb, basketball slam-dunk champ, is named not after the tuber, but in honor of "Sputnik," the Soviet satellite launched in his infancy.

YAM   Clarence Yaryan *catcher*
CARROTS[4]   Lillian Gish *actress*
SPINACH   Oscar Melillo *Browns infielder, aka "Ski," "The Little Wop"*
THE BEAN   Coleman Hawkins *jazz sax immortal*
BUTTERBEAN   Bob Love *basketball player*
STRINGBEAN   David Akeman *country singer*
PEAHEAD   (see Head to Toe [Heads])
SQUASH   Frank Wilson *Braves outfielder 1924–28*
THE GALLATIN SQUASH   Hub Perdue *Braves pitcher 1911–15*
CUKE   Roland Barrows *outfielder 1909–12*
TOMATOES   Frank "Jake" Kafora *catcher 1913–14*
TOMATO FACE, OLD TOMATO FACE   (see Head to Toe [Faces])
PICKLES[5]   William Dillhoefer *catcher* / George Gerken *outfielder* / John H. Heinz
   U.S. senator
CORNCOB   Jerry Reichow *football player*
SPIRO T. EGGPLANT   Spiro T. Agnew *Nixon's veep*
THE TURNIP HOER   George I *king of England 1714–27*
THE ARTICHOKE KING   Ciro Terranova *mobster*

Fruits

FRUIT   Morris White *guitarist*
PEACHES[6]   Frances Browning *flapper* / Ray Davis *pitcher* / Linda Greene *singer*
   (of "Peaches and Herb")
THE DELAWARE PEACH   Vic Willis *pitcher*
THE GEORGIA PEACH   Ty Cobb *Tiger slugger, speedster, Hall of Famer*
STRAWBERRY BILL   William Bernhard *pitcher 1899–1907*
CRANBERRY   Charles L. Gifford *Massachusetts politician* / Joan Crawford (Lucille
   Le Sueur) *actress, tycoon, mother*
CHERRY NOSE, BANANA NOSE   (see Head to Toe [Noses])
BANANA   Lowell Levinger *jazz musician*
BANANAS   Joe Benes *infielder*
JOE BANANAS   Joseph Bonanno *Mafia "Don," Man of Honor*
GRAPEFRUIT   Wilbert Robinson *aka "Uncle Robbie," catcher, manager*
APPLES   Andy Lapihuska *Phillies pitcher 1942–43*
JOHNNY APPLESEED   (John Chapman) *pioneer, farmer, land speculator*

4. Carrots. Miss Gish insisted on a plentiful supply of these in her dressing room—for nutritional purposes, we assume.
5. Pickles. With last names like Gerken and Dillhoefer, the tag is inevitable. Senator Heinz is a scion of the condiment dynasty.
6. Peaches. Frances Browning divorced millionaire "Daddy" Browning in 1927, and the NYC tabloids made the most of the scandal, taking special delight in their nicknames for each other.

APPLE CHEEKS   Harry Lumley *hockey goalie, Hall of Famer*
THE CRABAPPLE COMET   Johnny Rucker *Giants outfielder 1940–46*
PRUNES   George H. Moolic *catcher 1886*
FIG   Robert Lee Newton *football back*
PIT   John Quinn *catcher (1 game, 1911)*
THE HAWAIIAN PINEAPPLE KING   James Dole *agrobusinessman*

Poultry

CHICKEN   Fred Stanley *infielder* / William Van Winkle Wolf *outfielder*
TURKEY   Joe Jones *football player*
TURKEY MIKE   Donlin *outfielder*
DUCK   Garland Shifflett *pitcher*
GOOSE   Leon Goslin *Senators slugger* / Rich Gossage *ace relief pitcher* / Reese
    Tatum *Harlem Globetrotter, aka "The Clown Prince of Basketball"*
JOHNNY EGGS   *alias of Meyer "The Bug" Lansky, crime "czar"*
EGGIE   James Edgar "Ed" Lennox *3rd baseman*
HUEVO   Vincente Romo *relief pitcher*

Grains

GRITS   (see Jimmy "Hots" Carter, U.S. Presidents)
OATS   Joe DeMaestri *shortstop 1951–61*
RICE   Gus Aiken *jazz trumpeter*
ALFALFA BILL   William H. Murray *politician*
ALFALFA   Carl Switzer *actor (Our Gang)*
FARINA   Alan Clayton Hoskins, Jr. *actor (Our Gang)*
BUCKWHEAT   William Henry Thomas *actor (Our Gang)*
BUCK WHEAT   Zachariah "Zack" Wheat *Dodger Hall of Famer*
PETIE WHEATSTRAW   (William Bunch) *blues singer*
TOAST   Elvis Patterson *often "burned" cornerback*
MOTSY   Phil Handler *football coach (it's short for "Matzoh")*
BROTHER CORNBREAD   Joe Thomas *jazz musician*
OLD BISCUIT PANTS   Lou Gehrig (see "The Durable Dutchman," Foreigners)
PANCAKE   Broderick Perkins *Padres 1st baseman*
THE HOTCAKE BARON   William Childs *restaurateur*

Sweets

SWEETS   Harry Edison *Ellington sideman*
SUGAR   Ultiminio Ramos *featherweight champ 1963–64*
SUGAR RAY   Leonard[7] *welterweight champ 1979–80* / Robinson (Walker Smith)
    middleweight champ 1958–60 / Seales *middleweight challenger 1979*

7. Sugar Ray Leonard was endowed with his nickname by Howard Cosell, in honor of
former champ Sugar Ray Robinson, whose real name was Walker Smith, anyway.

SUGAR BOY   Joseph "Po' Joe" Williams *singer*
SUGAR[8] CAIN   Bob Cain, Merritt Cain *pitchers*
SUGARCANE   Don Harris *hot violinist*
SUGAR KANE   Katherine Kane *actress* / Frank Kane, Tom Kane *baseball players*
BROWN SUGAR   Lucille "Lil" Armstrong *singer, Satchmo's wife*
HONEY   John Barnes *Yankee 1926* / Billy Mellody *welterweight champ 1906–07*
HONI   Charles Coles *actor, singer, dancer (formerly "Honey")*
HONEY BOY   David Edwards *blues singer*
HONEY FITZ   John F. Fitzgerald *patriarch*
THE HONEYDRIPPER   (see Love & Sex)
CANDY   William Cummings *Hall of Fame pitcher*
LOLLYPOP   Wade "Red" Killefer *fielding brother of catcher "Reindeer Bill"*
THE LOLLIPOP GOVERNOR   Bill "Boyscout" Milliken *politician*
PEPPERMINT   Alfonso Frazer *junior middleweight champ 1972* / Harris (Harrison Nelson) *musician*
THE LICORICE LASHER   (see "The Brown Bomber," Assorted Mayhem)
KID CHOCOLATE (THE CUBAN BON BON)   Seligio Sardinias *featherweight champ 1933*
LITTLE CHOCOLATE   George Dixon *fighter*
CHOCOLATE THUNDER   (see "Earthquake," Weather)
TAFFY   Taft Wright *outfielder 1938–49*
COOKIE   Charles Cook *tap dancer* / Earl Gilchrist *football halfback* / Harry Lavagetto *pinch-hitting great*
BROWNIE   Walter McGhee *bluesman*
DOUGHNUT   Bill Carrick *Dodger pitcher (lost 22 in 1900)*
PIE   John McKenzie *Bruins hockey player* / Harold Traynor *Pirates shortstop*
PEACH PIE   Jack O'Connor *catcher 1887–1910*
SWEET BREADS   Abe Baily *pitcher*
JELLY ROLL[9]   Ferdinand Morton *jazz pianist, singer*
JELLO BIAFRA   (Eric Boucher) *singer (The Dead Kennedys)*
CHEWING GUM[10]   John O'Brien *infielder*
THE BLINTZ PRINCE   Bob Sherman *restaurateur*

---

8. Sugar. Another "inevitable" with last names Kane, Cain, Cane, etc. Like "Fig" Newton, "Goose" Goslin, etc. (see above).

9. Jelly Roll. For some curious reason, a nickname for the male organ of generation (in blues songs). Morton claimed with some justification to have invented jazz while playing piano in a New Orleans cat house. "Jazz" itself is a nickname for the product of the above-mentioned organ, as well as the process whereby said product is obtained.

10. Chewing Gum. O'Brien was that relative rarity, a Canadian-born major-league ballplayer. In Canada nicknames like "Chewing Gum" are considered racy. Other Canuck examples: George "Twinkletoes" Selkirk, Charles "Goody" Rosen, Edward "Tip" O'Neill (see After Dinner, below).

Condiments

SALT   David Walther *car racer*
SALTY   Francis Parker *baseball player*
PEPPER   Park Adams *sax player* / James Austin *baseball coach* / Johnny Martin
 infielder, aka "The Wild Hoss of the Osage"
BITTER HERB   Herb Ross *pitcher*
GINGER   Rogers (Virginia McMath) *dancer, actress*
VINEGAR   Joe Stilwell *U.S. general*
VINEGAR BEND   Wilmer Mizell *pitcher*
OIL   Earl Smith *catcher*
THE TABASCO KID   Norman "Kid" Elberfeld *baseball manager*
CURRY   Charles Foley *pitcher, outfielder 1879–83*
MSG   *Madison Square Garden*

The Kitchen

REFRIGERATOR   William Perry *football legend*
ICEBOX   Elton Chamberlain *pitcher 1886–96*
DEEP FREEZE WOMAN   Dorothy May Stevens Anderson *revived blizzard victim*
KETTLE   Elwood Wirtz *catcher*
POT   Frank LaPorte *2nd baseman*
SPOON   Jimmy Witherspoon *musician*
SPOONS   Benjamin "The Beast" Butler *Union general, accused of stealing cutlery*
CAP THE KNIFE   Caspar Weinberger *secretary of defense*

After Dinner

VITAMIN   Verda Smith *football running back*
SEN-SEN   John P. J. Sensenderfer *center fielder 1871–74, aka "Count"*
TOOTHPICK   Samuel Jones *pitcher, aka "Sad Sam"*
THE CIGAR   Carmine "Lilo" Galante *gangster, aka "Boss of Bosses"*
TAB   Talmadge Smith *musician*
TIP   Thomas P. O'Neill *Speaker of the House* / James Edward O'Neill *baseball star*
TIPPER[11]   Mary Elizabeth (Aitcheson) Gore *wife of Senator Albert Gore*

Name Your Poison Department

DRINK

BRANDY   Robert Brandon Davis *baseball player*
SHERRY   Sherwood Magee, Sherrad Smith *baseball players*

---

11. Tipper. Special thanks for this info to Jimbo "Deep Throat" Todd, of Al's office.

CHAMPAGNE   Evelyn King *pop singer* / Tony Lema *golfer*
WHISKEY   Billy Kilmer *quarterback*
BLOODY MARY   Mary Tudor *Queen of Scots (the drink was named for her)*
THE BOILERMAKER   James J. Jeffries *heavyweight champ 1899–1905, aka "The California Hercules"*
HARD CIDER   (see William "Tippecanoe" Harrison, U.S. Presidents)
HIGHBALL   Howard Wilson *baseball player*
RED EYE   James Hay *hockey player*
SOUR MASH   Harold Jack Daniels *baseball player*
DOUBLE X   Jimmy "The Beast" Foxx *baseball player*
HALF PINT RYE   Gene Rye *baseball player*
SUDS   Gene Fodge, Bill Sudakis *baseball players*
KEG   Frederick Johnson *jazz musician* / William Purnell *drummer*
BREWERY   Jack Taylor *pitcher*
BREW   Milton Moore *tenor sax player*
JUG   Eugene Ammons *sax player*
JUGHANDLE JOHNNY   Johnny Morrison *baseball player*
JIGGER   Arnold Statz *baseball player*
CORK   Ted Wilks *pitcher*
SIPPIE[1]   Beulah Wallace *blues singer*
KING OF THE MOONSHINERS   W. R. Gooch *distiller*
HERO OF MANY A HARD-FOUGHT BOTTLE   (see Pierce, U.S. Presidents)
THE DRUNKEN TAILOR   (see Andy Johnson, U.S. Presidents)
EGBERT SOUSE   *(read Sousé) pseudonym of W. C. Fields*
THE KANSAS DRY   U.S. Guyer *prohibitionist*
BOBBY MILK   Robert DeNiro *actor (as a puny child)*
BUTTERMILK   Tommy Dowd *baseball player*
COCOA   Dan Woodman *baseball player*
BOSCO   Colonel Snover *baseball player*
PUNCH   Lyle Judy *baseball player* / Ernest Miller Sulzberger *publisher*
THE COCA-COLA GIRL, THE CHAMPAGNE GIRL   (see The Girls)
SASSAFRAS   George Winter *pitcher*
JUICE   George Latham *baseball player*
THE JUICE   O. J. (Orenthál James) Simpson *football player*
GRAPE JUICE   Greg Johnson *football, track star*
SWEET JUICE   William Johnson *baseball player*
ICED TEA   Howard Johnson *baseball player, aka "Hojo"*
EARL GREY   Bob Dylan (see "Blind Boy Grunt," Head to Toe [Gimps])
LEMONADE LUCY   Mrs. Rutherford B. Hayes *first lady, temperance advocate*
COLD WATER JIM   James Hughey *pitcher*

---

1. Sippie. The late singer's name is, of course, an abbreviation of Mississippi—but we thought it went nicely here.

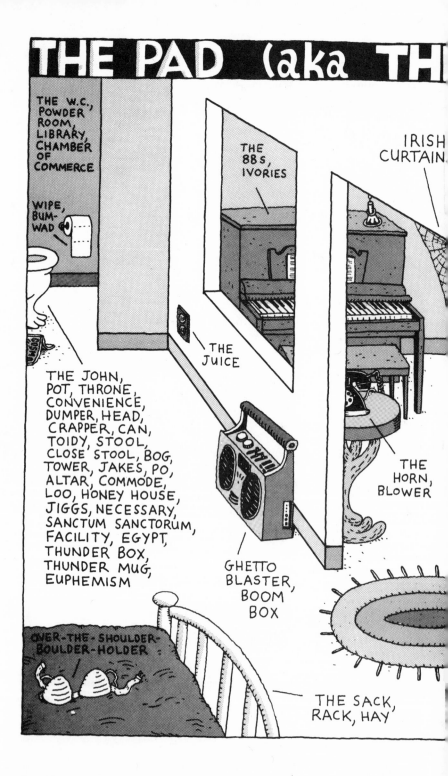

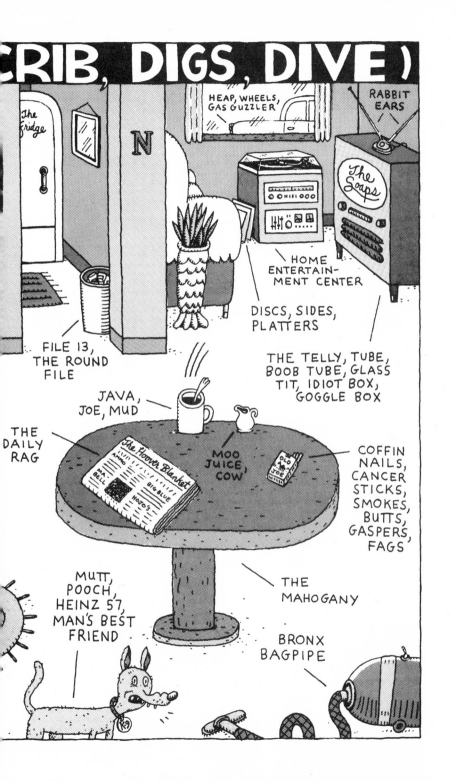

4
WORK HARD, PLAY HARD

Call It in the Air Department

MONEY

If a man has no nickname, he never grows rich.

—Chinese proverb

A Good Name is worth more than Riches.
—The Bible, aka Holy Scripture, The Good Book, Holy Writ, etc.

MONEY   Harold Johnson *flugelhorn player*
CASH   Joseph "Bill" Taylor *outfielder*
CASH AND CARRY   C. C. Pyle *entrepreneur*
OLD BULLION, GOLD BUG   Thomas Hart Benton *Missouri senator, aka "Old Humbug"*
MR. ECONOMY   Harry "Curly" Byrd *Virginia senator*
PAYROLL   Bess Truman *first lady*
JOHNNY PAYCHECK   (Donald Lytle) *country singer, aka "Ohio Kid"*
TRIPLE SCALE   Tom Scott *musician (doesn't work for scale)*
STOCKS   Wally Stocking *fighter*
GARY U.S. BONDS   Gary Bonds *singer, musician*
THE JUNK BOND KING   Michael Milken *financier*
THE BAREFOOT BOY OF WALL STREET   Wendell L. Willkie *politician*
THE WITCH OF WALL STREET[1]   Hetty Green *financier*
THE MAN WHO BROKE THE BANK AT MONTE CARLO   Charles Wells *famed gambler of song*
MONEY BAGS   Tom Qualters *baseball player*

1. Witch of Wall Street. Hannah "Hetty" Green (1834–1916) was the richest woman in the U.S. in her time. She dressed and behaved like a "bag lady," helping to establish the myth of the bum with his mattress stuffed with money.

THE BIG BANKROLL   Arnold Rothstein (see "Mr. Big," Size)

DADDY BIG BUCKS   (see "The Phantom Angel," Religion & Mystery)

JAKOB THE RICH   Jakob Fugger *16th-century German banker*

TYCOON   (see "Honest Abe" Lincoln, U.S. Presidents)

OWNEY   Owen Madden *murderer, bootlegger*

THE MEAL TICKET   "King" Carl Hubbell *Hall of Fame pitcher, aka "The Meek Man from Meeker"*

POOR LITTLE RICH GIRL   Barbara Hutton *heiress*

THE MILLION DOLLAR BABY FROM THE 5 & 10 CENT STORE   Lewis "Hack" Wilson *baseball player*

BET A MILLION   John Wayne Gates *promoter, gambler*

THE $10,000 BEAUTY   Mike "King" Kelly *baseball Hall of Famer*

ONE GRAND   Ernest J. Schmidt *basketball Hall of Famer*

SAWBUCK   Sears Roebuck *(compare "Monkey Ward")*

DOLLAR   Bill Bradley *New Jersey senator* / Adolphus Brand (Abdullah Ibrahim) *jazz pianist* / John Lang *NY gambler, circa 1910*

BUCK² Wilbur Clayton *musician* / Walter Leonard *baseball Hall of Famer* / Alvis Owens *country musician* / etc.

JINGLE MONEY   James Smith *embezzler*

TEN CENT JIMMY   (see Jimmy Buchanan, U.S. Presidents)

FIVE-CENT CIGAR³ Thomas R. Marshall *Wilson's veep*

PENNY   Fred Bailey *baseball player*

SLUG   Harry Heilmann *baseball Hall of Famer*

COUSIN CHEAP   Hugh Carter, Jr. *Jimmy's cousin*

CUT RATE   Terry M. Carpenter *Nebraska politician*

ZERO   Samuel Mostel *actor*

MADAME DEFICIT   Marie Antoinette *guillotined 1793*

POOR RICHARD   Benjamin Franklin *statesman, inventor, publisher, aka "Tamer of Lightning"*

PO' JOE   Joseph "Sugar Boy" Williams *singer*

POOR MAN'S FRIEND   James Couzens *Michigan politician, aka "Croesus of the Senate"*

MOOCHIE   Freddie "The Flea" Patek *baseball player* / Marlon Starling *welterweight fighter*

---

2. Buck. "Fat black bucks in a wine barrel room" is the way poet Vachel Lindsay described a gathering of Afro-Americans. "Buck" meant young black man, son of a "Mammy" and potential father of a "sucker." In the case of redneck country singer Buck Owens, of course, it's short for "buckaroo."

3. Five-Cent Cigar. It was during an especially tedious nominating speech at a Democratic convention that free-spirit Marshall observed that "What this country needs is a good five-cent cigar" within earshot of a reporter.

If You Call That Working Department

PROFESSIONS

THE CHAIRMAN OF THE BOARD   Edward "Whitey" Ford *baseball Hall of Famer* / Frank "Ol' Blue Eyes" Sinatra *singer, aka "The Voice," "Swoonatra"*

BOSS OF BOSSES   Carmine "Lilo" Galante *gangster, aka "The Cigar"*

THE BOSS   Bruce Springsteen *rock singer*

BOSS   Richard J. Daley *Chicago mayor* / Florence Harding *first lady* / Tweed (see "The Tammany Tiger," Mammals)

EASY BOSS   Thomas C. "Me Too" Platt *politician*

PRES   Lester Young *sax great, aka "Porkpie Hat"*

VEEP   Alben Barkley *Truman's VP*

THE SENATOR   Grimes (See "Ol' Stubble Beard," Head to Toe [Hair])

GOVERNOR   Frank Ellerbee *baseball player*

ALDERMAN   Charles "Fatty" Briody *baseball player*

THE OLD PERFESSOR   Charles "Casey" Stengel *baseball Hall of Famer*

THE LITTLE PROFESSOR   Dom DiMaggio *outfielder*

PROFESSOR   Irwin Corey *comedian* / John Duffy *ring referee* / Woody "Doc" Wilson (see U.S. Presidents)

PROFESSOR BACKWARDS   (James Edmundson) *specialty comedian*

PROFESSOR LONGHAIR[1]   (Harold Roeland Byrd) *musician*

THE TEACHER PRESIDENT   (see "Canal Boy" James Garfield, U.S. Presidents)

THE GOSHEN SCHOOLMASTER   Sam Leever *pitcher*

LEARNED BLACKSMITH   Elihu Burritt *linguist, reformer*

FARMER BOB   Robert "Muley" Doughton, Robert Scott *politicians*

THE PEANUT FARMER   (see Jimmy "Hots" Carter, U.S. Presidents)

THE TURNIP HOER   George I *king of England 1714–27*

THE TENNESSEE PLOWBOY   Eddie Arnold *singer*

WHEAT PICKER   J. D. Smith *football player*

LITTLE MISS SHARECROPPER   LaVern Baker *singer*

THE RAILSPLITTER   (see "Honest Abe" Lincoln, U.S. Presidents)

THE CHICKEN PLUCKER   Bobby Riggs *tennis misfit*

THE SINGING BRAKEMAN   Jimmy Rogers *country music great*

THE SINGING RANGER   Clarence "Hank" Snow *singer*

THE SINGING FISHERMAN   Johnny Horton *pop star*

THE MAD MACKEREL MERCHANT   Battling Levinsky (Barney Lebrowitz) *light heavyweight boxer, aka "The Furious Fishmonger"*

ICE MAN   Bob Coolidge *fighter* / George Woolf *jockey*

THE ICE MAN   Jerry Butler *soul and gospel singer* / George Gervin *basketball player* / Ben "Bantam" Hogan *golf great*

1. Professor was an honorific applied to all whorehouse (and burlesque house) piano players, "Longhair" being the last of the breed.

BUTCHER BOY   Charles Schmidt *3rd baseman* / Carl Wanderer *wife killer*
THE BAKER   George Millsom *heavyweight champ 1762–65*
THE BARBER   Sal Maglie *"brushback" pitcher*
MILKMAN JIM   Jim Turner *pitcher*
THE WAITER   Paul Lucca *gangster*
THE MAIL CARRIER   Earle "The Kentucky Colonel" Combs *baseball Hall of Famer*
THE GARBAGE MAN   Steve Shutt *Montreal Canadiens rebound specialist*
THE GROCER   Edward Heath *British PM*
THE PHARMACIST   John Zaccaro, Jr. *Gerry's kid*
FIREMAN   Joe Page *baseball player, aka "The Pitching Poet"*
THE ACTOR   Willie Sutton *bank robber*
THE OLD LAMPLIGHTER   Hector "Toe" Blake *hockey player, coach*
CORONER   J. O. Fernandez *Louisiana politician, aka "Deadhead"*
THE UNDERTAKER   Leonard Woodcock *labor leader*
THE BROWN EMBALMER   (see "The Brown Bomber," Assorted Mayhem)
DIGGER   Richard Phelps *basketball coach* / George Stanley *fighter*
THE NEWSBOY[2]   Abe Hollandersky *fighter*
THE MESSENGER   "Buffalo" Bill Cody *scout*
PEDLAR   Thomas Palmer *fighter, aka "Little Box of Tricks"*
SPACEMAN   Bill Lee *left-handed pitcher and "flake"*
MINER   Mordecai "Three Finger" Brown *Hall of Fame pitcher*
THE LOCKSMITH KING   Louis XVI *king of France 1774–93*
ALEXANDER THE COPPERSMITH   Alexander Hamilton *1st secretary of the treasury, aka "Little Lion"*
THE SURVEYOR *OR* FARMER PRESIDENT   (see Washington, U.S. Presidents)
THE HABERDASHER   (see "Give 'em Hell" Harry Truman, U.S. Presidents)
THE DRUNKEN TAILOR   (see Andy Johnson, U.S. Presidents)
THE PRODUCTION LINE   Detroit Redwings, '50s (Howe, Abel, Lindsey)
THE LUMBER COMPANY   Pittsburgh Pirates, '80s (Pop Stargell, Cobra Parker)
THE NEW YORK SACK EXCHANGE   *New York Jets pass defense*
UNION MAN   Walter Holke *Giants, Braves, Phillies 1st baseman 1914–25*
OLD 8 TO 7   (see Rutherford B. "Granny" Hayes, U.S. Presidents)
FOUR-JOB FARLEY   James A. Farley *dollar-a-year-man in FDR's cabinet*
THE HARDEST WORKING MAN IN SHOW BUSINESS   (see "Mr. Dynamite," Misters)
MEMO   Guillermo Luna *pitcher, 1954 Cards*
BUM   Oail Phillips *football coach*

(See also: Crime & Punishment, Religion & Mystery, The Military)

---

2. The Newsboy. Abe Hollandersky took part in a (record) 1,309 pro fights. He is not to be confused with Newsboy Brown, defeated by Panama Al Brown for the bantamweight title in 1931.

Call Me a Doctor Department

DOCTORS

DR. A   Al Silverstein *syndicated medical columnist*
DR. BUZZARD   August Darnell *musician, better known as "Kid Creole"*
DR. CLOCK   Mickey Cobb *baseball trainer*
DR. DEMENTO   (Barry Hanson) *deejay*
DR. DIRT   Tim Wilkison *tennis player, aka "Rambo"*
DR. DUNKENSTEIN   Darrell Griffith *basketball player*
DR. HIP   Eugene Schoenfield *underground press medical columnist*
DR. HOOK   (Dennis Locorriere) *pop singer*
DR. J   Julius Erving *basketball great*
DR. JAZZ   Dennis Zeitlin *pianist and physician*
DR. JIVE   Tommy Smalls *musician*
DR. JOHN   (Mac Rebbenack) *musician, singer*
DR. K   Dwight Gooden *Mets pitcher*
DR. NO   Harold Brown *U.S. secretary of defense*
DR. ROCK   Harrison "Jack" Schmitt *astronaut-geologist*
DR. SCOLD   Johnnie "Dusty" Baker *baseball player*
DR. SEUSS   (Theodore Geisel) *author, illustrator*
DR. STRANGELOVE, DR. STRANGEGLOVE (see Cartoon & Other Literary Figures)
ADMIRABLE DOCTOR   Roger Bacon *philosopher*
THE ANGELIC DOCTOR   Thomas Aquinas *theologian*
THE JUNGLE DOCTOR   Thomas Dooley *missionary*
DOC   Frank Bagley *fight manager* / Felix "Mr. Inside" Blanchard *football player* / Adolphus Cheatham *trumpeter* / Carl H. Severinsen *trumpeter, bandleader* / Neil Simon *playwright* / Arthel Watson *guitarist, singer* / Woody Wilson (see U.S. Presidents) / etc.
BABY DOC   Jean-Claude Duvalier *deposed Haitian dictator, aka "Baskethead"*
PAPA DOC   François Duvalier *father of the baby*
MEDICINE BILL   Billy Mountjoy *pitcher 1883–85*

Tag, You're It Department

SPORTS & RECREATION

SPORT   George Bucher *gangster*
POLO   Stan Andrews *baseball player* / Paul Barnes *clarinetist*
SQUASH   Frank Wilson *baseball player*
SKI   Oscar Melillo *infielder, aka "Spinach," "The Little Wop"*

SKI NOSE   Bob "For Texaco" Hope (Leslie Townes Hope) *comedian, actor, boxed under the name "Packy East"*

SNOW SHOE   Jimmy Thompson *pioneer*

TENNIS BALL HEAD   Steve Hovley *outfielder 1969–73*

NATE THE SKATE   Nate "Tiny" Archibald *basketball player*

MURPH THE SURF   Jack Roland Murphy *burglar, evangelist*

THE SWIMMING NUN   Stella Taylor *athlete*

THE VAULTING VICAR   Bob Richards *Olympic track star*

THE HUMAN BOWLING BALL   Don Nottingham *football player*

BOCCI   Ernie "Schnozz" Lombardi *baseball Hall of Famer*

SKEETS   Richard Gallagher *comedian* / William Burke Miller *reporter* / Renaldo Nehemia *track, football star*

CLAY PIGEON   (see "Legs Diamond," Head to Toe [Extremities])

TEDDY BALLGAME   (see "The Splendid Splinter," Wood & Fire)

HOME RUN   Joe Marshall *home-runless player* / Jerry Smith [1] *football player*

JOCKEY   Bibb Falk *outfielder*

DERBY DAY   Bill Clymer *baseball player*

QUARTERBACK   *General Stilwell's WWII code name*

THE GREAT GOLFER   (see Dwight D. "Ike" Eisenhower, U.S. Presidents)

GOLF BAG   Sam Hunt *criminal (carried a shotgun in his golf bag)*

GOLFBALL   Dolphus Hull *caddie*

TEE   Clarence Carpenter *fighter*

BOGIE   Humphrey Bogart *movie actor*

BIRDIE, EAGLE   (see Birds)

MICKEY MANTLE'S CADDIE   Ross Moschitto *baseball player*

KITE   Keith Thomas *baseball player*

KNITTING   Hattie Caraway *political widow turned politician (Iowa senator)*

PEEK-A-BOO   (see Head to Toe [Eyes, Vision])

BINGO   Bobby Smith *basketball player*

CHUBBY CHECKER   (see Size)

THE TOY CANNON   Jim Wynn *baseball player*

YO-YO   Pompeyo Davalillo *baseball player*

DOLLEY   Dorothea Madison *first lady*

KEWPIE DAHL   Percival Dahl *football player*

KEWPIE   Johnny Ertle *fighter*

CABBAGE PATCH   Wally Backman *baseball player*

CIRCUS SOLLY   Arthur "Solly" Hofman *baseball player*

KING OF THE FAIRS   Carlos Figueroa *harness-horse trainer*

SYMPHONY SID   Sid Torin *deejay*

---

1. Home Run. Redskins coach Allen gave this nickname to halfback Smith, who became, in 1986, the first pro athlete victim of AIDS.

Call Me Ishmael Department

CARTOON & OTHER LITERARY FIGURES

SMURF   David M. Smith *cricket player*

MICKEY MOUSE   Mickey Melten *baseball player*

DONALD DUCK   Donald Bailey *trumpet player* / Donald Dunn *bass player*

GOOFY   Vernon "Lefty" Gomez *Hall of Fame pitcher*

BAMBI   Lance Alworth *football player*

THUMPER   (see "The Splendid Splinter," Wood & Fire)

PINOCCHIO   James Cornelius *jazz singer*

THE CINDERELLA MAN   James J. Braddock *heavyweight champ 1935–37*

DOC (see Doctors)/SLEEPY, BASHFUL, HAPPY, GRUMPS, DOPESTER (see Attitudes)

POPEYE   William E. Simon *secretary of the treasury*

WIMPY   Jerry Halstead *fighter* / Tom Paciorek *baseball player*

SWEE' PEA   Billy Strayhorn *composer, musician*

THE BETTY BOOP GIRL   Mae Questal *actress*

BUGS   (see Insects)

FUD   Joe Livingston *clarinetist*

PORKY   Edward S. Oliver *golfer* / Hal Reniff *catcher*

DAFFY   Paul Dean *pitcher, brother of "Dizzy"*

THE ROAD RUNNER   Yvon Cournoyer *hockey player*

SPEEDY GONZALEZ   José Gonzalez, Zeferino Gonzalez *fighters*

YOGI[1]   Lawrence Peter Berra *baseball player, manager*

BOO BOO   Paul Palmer *college football player*

TOP CAT   Cubby Jackson *jazz musician*

TOM AND JERRY   *stage name of young Simon and Garfunkel*

GERALD McBOING-BOING   Anthony Cahan *surgeon*

TOM TERRIFIC   Tom Seaver *pitcher*

PEBBLES   Walter Rock *football player*

SNUFFY SMITH   Clinton Smith *hockey player*

MOON MULLENS   Edward Mullens *trumpet player*

BEETLE BAILEY   Robert S. Bailey *baseball player*

LI'L ABNER   Paul Erickson *baseball player* / Cliff Hagen *basketball player*

LITTLE NEMO   James Stephens *baseball player*

SMOKEY STOVER   William Stover McIlwain *baseball player*

THE YELLOW KID   Joseph Weil *Chicago con man*

MANDRAKE THE MAGICIAN   Don Mueller *baseball player*

PEANUTS   (see Food [Appetizers])

PIGPEN   Ron McKerran *musician*

1. Yogi. Alone in this list, Berra has the distinction of having had a cartoon character—Yogi Bear—named after *him*.

JIGGS   Hayden Whigham *trombone player*
MUMBLES   Bill Tremel *pitcher*
BATMAN   Tony Ortega *fighter*
THE BOY WONDER   Stanley Harris *baseball player*
TARZAN   Charles Cooper *basketball Hall of Famer*
THE SPIRIT   Mickey Davis *basketball player*
THE PHANTOM   Julian Javier *baseball player*
THE SPIDERMAN RAPIST   Tyrone Graham *criminal fire escape climber*
FLASH GORDON, THE GREEN HORNET   General George S. Patton *aka "Old Blood and Guts," "The Old Man"*
PAPA BEAR   George Halas *founder, head coach, Chicago Bears*
LITTLE BEAU PEEP, THE BIG BLAB WOLF   Walter "Big Ear" Winchell *columnist, aka "Vulture Vinchell," "Keyhole Winchell," "The Great Gabbo"*
JACK THE GIANT KILLER   Jack Dempsey (see "The Manassa Mauler," Assorted Mayhem) / Jack Dillon (Ernest Cutler Price) *light heavyweight champ*
THE MAD HATTER   Albert Anastasia *hitman, aka "The Lord High Executioner"*
KING LEAR   Charles Lear, Fred Lear *baseball players*
SAMSON   Harlin Pool *outfielder*
HERCULES   Mary Promitis *marathon dance champ*
THE CALIFORNIA HERCULES   (see "The Boilermaker," Drink)
THE PRUSSIAN LEPRECHAUN   Frank Leahy *North Dakota football coach*
GENERAL TOM THUMB   Charles S. Straton *circus performer*
CAPTAIN HOOK   George "Sparky" Anderson *baseball player, manager*
LONG JEAN SILVER[2]   Jean Silver *one-legged porn star*
ALI BABA   A. J. Babartsky *football player*
THE 40 THIEVES   *New York City's Board of Aldermen, circa 1860*
PRINCE ARTHUR   (see Chet "The Dude" Arthur, U.S. Presidents)
CAMELOT   *the Kennedy White House*
THE ROUND TABLE   *the Algonquin's famed literati patrons*
KNIGHT OF THE RED ROSE   Alfred A. "Uncle Alf" Taylor *Tennessee governor and congressman*
KNIGHT OF THE WHITE ROSE   Robert L. "Fiddling Bob" Taylor *Tennessee governor and senator*
THE DRAGON LADY   Madame Ngo Dinh Nhu *power-wielding sister-in-law of former S. Vietnam president Ngo Dinh Diem*
GULLIVER   Paul Lehner *outfielder*
THE ARTFUL DODGER   Dave Needham *British featherweight*
TINY TIM   (Howard Khaury) *entertainer*
TOM JONES   (Thomas Woodward) *singer*
ENGELBERT HUMPERDINCK (Arnold Dorsey) *singer*

---

2. Long Jean Silver. Appeared in *Pleasure Island* and *Stump the Band.*

YOUNG CASANOVA   Hector Medina *fighter*
UNCLE TOM   Thomas Bannon *baseball player*
THE BOSTON TAR BABY   Sam Langford *fighter*
THE ANCIENT MARINER   Gaylord Perry *pitcher*
MR. CHIPS   Bob Chipman *pitcher*
THE STRANGER   Bill Walton *basketball player*
THE MAN WITH THE GOLDEN ARM   Sandy Koufax *pitcher*
HARRY THE HORSE   Harry Danning *baseball player*
SANDMAN   Clayman Parker *fighter*
DR. STRANGELOVE   Edward Teller *physicist*
DR. STRANGEGLOVE   Dick Stuart *error-prone baseball star*
THE WIZARD OF OZ   Ozzie Smith *shortstop*
THE WIZARD OF OOZE   Everett M. Dirksen *senator*
CHARLIE CHAN   alias of Charlie "Bird" Parker *sax great*
RAMBO   Tim "Dr. Dirt" Wilkison *tennis player*
BRUCE LEE   Fred Basa *Filipino flyweight*
BEN TURPIN   C. Murray Turpin *Pennsylvania politician*
TOM MIX   Salvatore Santoro *crime underboss*
THE DRACULA SLUMLORD OF FLATBUSH   J. Leonard Spodek *landlord*
QUEEN OF THE VAMPIRES   (see "The Original Glamour Girl," The Girls)
WOLFMAN JACK   (Robert Smith) *radio personality*
KING KONG   Charlie Keller *baseball player* / Caifas Masondo *fighter*
KONG   Dave Kingman *baseball player*
BONZO   John Bonham *drummer*
BOZO   Sterling Bose *trumpet player* / James Shupe *gangster*
BIG BIRD   Mark "The Bird" Fidrych *pitcher*
TOPO GIGIO   Manuel Vasquez *Mexican bantamweight*
PUNCH JUDY   Lyle Judy *baseball player*
BOCEPHUS   Hank Williams, Jr. *singer, named for the local TV puppet he resembled as a child*
TOPPER   Emory Rigby *shortstop*
ZORRO   Zoilo Versalles *baseball player*
BIONIC BILL   William J. Schroeder *lived 620 days with an artificial heart*
WARD   Ed Hearn *baseball player (after Ward Cleaver, Beaver's dad)*
WOJO   Randy Myers *baseball player (after a character on "Barney Miller")*
AMAZING GRACE   Grace Hopper *U.S. admiral, ret.*
OLD MAN RIVER   Archie "The Old Mongoose" Moore *light heavyweight champ 1952–60*
MACK THE KNIFE   Mack Jones *baseball player*
LITTLE BOY BLUE   "Little Albie" Booth *football player, aka "The Mighty Mite"*
KING COLE   Leonard Cole *pitcher*
ROCKETS' REDGLARE   (Michael Gennarro Morra) *actor, comedian*

ALL-STAR NICKNAME JAZZ BAND

SAX

1. 'TRANE (John Coltrane)
2. BIRD (Charlie Parker)
3. BEAN (Coleman Hawkins)
4. CANNONBALL (Julian Adderley)
5. FATHEAD (David Newman)

TRUMPET

6. BOZO (Sterling Bose)
7. BUNNY (Rowland Berigan)
8. DONALD DUCK (Donald Bailey)
9. PIKE (Clifton Davis)

PIANO

10. RAM (Roger Ramirez)
11. THE LION (Willie Smith)

12. JELLY ROLL (Ferdinand Morton)
13. COW COW (Charles Davenport)
14. MULE (Perry Bradford)

DRUMS

15. BUGS (John Hamilton)
16. BABY (Warren Dodds)

TROMBONE

17. MUTTONLEG (Ted Donnelly)

SINGER

18. HOWLIN' WOLF (Chester Burnett)

5

US AND THEM

Name Your State Department

THE 50 & DENIZENS

IOWA: named for the Ioway Indians, variously translated as "beautiful land," or "sleepy people" and "people who put people to sleep."

These are *authentic* nicknames of the States and their denizens. They have legendary, venerable histories (or else they're blazoned on Chamber of Commerce letterheads). Don't blame us. Check it out in G. E. Shankle's *State Names,* or Kane and Alexander's *Nicknames and Sobriquets of U.S. Cities, States and Counties.*

STATE	NICKNAME	CITIZENS
Alabama	The Lizard State	Yaller Hammers
Alaska	Uncle Sam's Icebox	Mushers
Arizona	One of America's Most Popular Playgrounds	Sandcutters
Arkansas	The Toothpick State	Goobergrabbers
California	The Grape State	Prunepickers
Colorado	Cupid's Hometown	
Connecticut	Land of Steady Habits, aka Where the Good Life Pays More in Corporate Dividends	Nutmegs
Delaware	Uncle Sam's Pocket Hankie	Muskrats
Florida	The Air-Conditioned State	Flies Up the Creek
Georgia	The Buzzard State	Crackers
Hawaii	Hulaland	
Idaho	The Place to Go	

Illinois	The Sucker State	Egyptians
Indiana	The Center of the Commercial Universe	Hoosiers
Iowa	The Food Market of the World	Hawkeyes
Kansas	The Squatter State	Grasshoppers
Kentucky	The Hemp State	Corncrackers
Louisiana	The Right-to-Profit State	Lousy-annas
Maine	Lobsterland	Maine-iacs
Maryland	The Oyster State	Crawthumpers
Massachusetts	The Bean Eating State	Puritans
Michigan	The Big Fish State	Wolverines
Minnesota	The Bread and Butter State, aka Cream Pitcher of the Nation	Gophers
Mississippi	The Mud Waddler State	Tadpoles
Missouri	The Puke State	Pikes
Montana	The Singed Cat State	Stub Toes
Nebraska	The Bug-Eating State	Bug-Eaters
Nevada	One Sound State	Diggers
New Hampshire	The Yankee Playground	Granite Boys
New Jersey	The Mosquito State	Spaniards
New Mexico	The Vermin State	Delightmakers
New York	The Knickerbocker State	New Yawkers
North Carolina	The Turpentine State	Tarboilers
North Dakota	Land of the North Furrow	Flickertails
Ohio	The Tomato State	Buckeyes
Oklahoma	The Boomers' Paradise	Okies
Oregon	The Webfoot State	Hardcases
Pennsylvania	The First State of Safety	Leatherheads
Rhode Island	Our Social Capital	Gunflints
South Carolina	The Iodine State, aka The Swamp State	Clayeaters
South Dakota	The Swing Cat State	
Tennessee	The Hog and Hominy State	Mudheads
Texas	America's Fun-tier	Beefheads
Utah	The Good Highway State	Polygamists
Vermont	Everybody's Second State	Green Mountain Boys
Virginia	The Virgin State, aka The Mother State	Sorebacks
Washington	The Fun State	Clamgrabbers
West Virginia	The Snake State	Panhandlers
Wisconsin	The Cheese Capital of the Nation	Badgers
Wyoming	The Land of Cattle and Sheep	Sheepherders

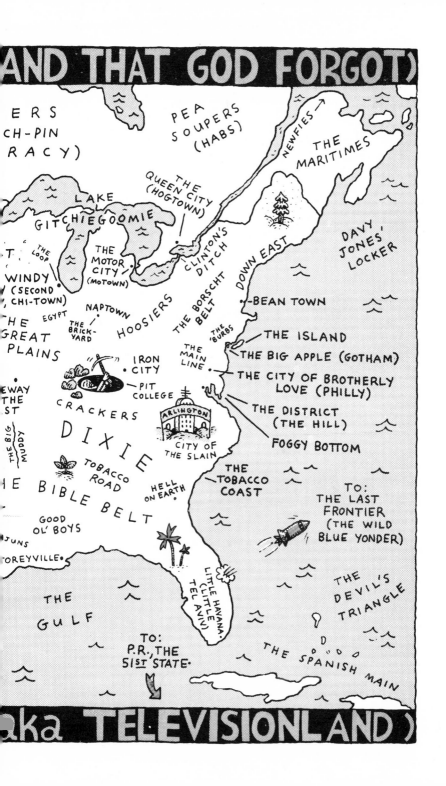

State Your Name Department

FAVORITE SONS

UNITED STATES, UNCLE SAM   (see "Butcher" Ulysses S. Grant, U.S. Presidents)

ALABAMA BLOSSOM   Guy Morton *Indians pitcher 1914–24*

ALABAM' ASSASSIN   (see "Brown Bomber," Assorted Mayhem)

ARIZONA DONNIE CLARK   *alias of Kate "Ma" Barker, criminal*

THE ARIZONA COWBOY   Rex Allen *western film star*

THE ARKANSAS HUMMINGBIRD   Lonnie Warnecke *C&W singer*

THE ARKANSAS HUNKERER   Wilbur Mills *senator*

THE ARKANSAS TRAVELER   Bob Burns *vaudeville comic*

THE CALIFORNIA HERCULES   James J. Jeffries *heavyweight champ 1899–1905*

THE CALIFORNIA MUSCLEMAN   (see "Madcap Maxie," Attitudes)

COLORADO CHICO   W. L. Rudd *soldier, frontiersman*

DAKOTA STATON   (Aliah Rabia) *songstress*

THE DELAWARE PEACH   Vic Willis *pitcher*

GEORGIA TOM   Tom Dorsey *bluesman*

THE GEORGIA DEACON   Theo "Tiger" Flowers *middleweight champ 1926–31*

THE GEORGIA PEACH   Tyrus "Ty" Cobb *aka "The Idol of Baseball Fandom"*

THE HAWAIIAN PINEAPPLE KING   James Dole *agrobusinessman*

THE IDAHO LION   (see "The Big Potato," Food)

ILLINOIS   Jean Baptiste Jacquet *jazz sax player*

THE ILLINOIS THUNDERBOLT   Ken Overlin *armed forces boxing champ*

INDIANA'S SONGBIRD   Helen Bucher *entertainer*

JERSEY JOE WALCOTT   (Arnold Cream) *heavyweight champ 1951–52*

THE JERSEY LILY   Lillie Langtry (Emilie Le Breton) *actress*

KANSAS   Carl Fields *drummer* / Joe McCoy *bluesman, married "Memphis Minnie"
(Lizzie Douglas)*

ROCKY KANSAS   (Rocco Tozzo) *fighter*

THE KENTUCKY COLONEL   Earle Combs *Yankee great, aka "The Mail Carrier"*

THE KENTUCKY RIFLE   Glen Combs *basketball star*

LOUISIANA'S   DICTATOR,   LOUISIANA'S   LOUD   SPEAKER   (see   "Kingfish,"
Assumed Titles)

LOUISIANA'S LIGHTNING   Ron "Gator" Guidry *Yankee pitcher*

THE MICHIGAN ASSASSIN   Stanley Ketchel (Stanislaus Kiecal) *middleweight
champ 1907–08*

THE MAN FROM MAINE   James G. Blaine (see "Uncrowned King," Assumed
Titles) / Edmund Muskie *senator and presidential hopeful*

THE MASSACHUSETTS GIANT   Daniel Webster *orator, statesman*

THE MICHIGAN WILDCAT   Ad Wolgast *lightweight champ 1910–12*

MINNESOTA FATS   (Rudolph Wanderone, Jr.) *pool shark*

MISSISSIPPI   John Hurt, Fred McDowell *bluesmen*

THE MADMAN FROM MISSISSIPPI   Gerald Walker *outfielder 1931–45, aka "Gee"*
MONTANA RED   (Don Tate) *rodeo rider*
MONTANA MIKE   Mike Mansfield *senator*
MONTANA SLIM   (Wilf Carter) *country singer*
SMALL MONTANA   (Benjamin Gan) *fighter*
NEVADA   Jack Rose *rodeo rider*
THE OHIO GONG   William "Foghorn" Allen *senator, aka "Rise-Up William,"*
   "Petticoat Allen"
OHIO KID   (Donald Lytle) *C&W singer, aka "Johnny Paycheck"*
OHIO FATS   Jack Nicklaus *golf great, aka "The Golden Bear"*
IDOL OF OHIO   (see McKinley, U.S. Presidents)
OKLAHOMA'S YODELING COWBOY   Gene Autry *actor, singer, entrepreneur*
THE OKLAHOMA PEDLAR   Albert S. Gilles *department store founder*
RHODY   Roderick Wallace *baseball Hall of Famer*
THE EAGLE ORATOR OF SOUTH CAROLINA   John C. Calhoun *statesman*
TENNESSEE   Ernie Ford *singer* / Thomas Lanier Williams *playwright*
THE TENNESSEE PLOWBOY   Eddie Arnold *Nashville star*
UTAH   Bruce Phillips *folk singer*
DINAH WASHINGTON   (Ruth Jones) *song stylist*
THE WEST VIRGINIA HILLBILLY   Sam Snead *golf great, aka "Slammin' Sammy"*
THE WISCONSIN WRATH   Russ Rebholz *football running back*

Native New Yorkers

LITTLE NEW YORK   Louis Campagna *criminal*
BROADWAY   Joe Namath *football QB* / Aleck Smith *baseball player*
THE KING OF BROADWAY   George M. Cohan *showman*
THE BRONX BOMBER   Alex Ramos *fighter*
THE BRONX BULL   Jacob "Jake" LaMotta *middleweight champ 1949–51*
THE DRACULA SLUMLORD OF FLATBUSH   J. Leonard Spodek *landlord*
THE DUKE OF FLATBUSH   Edwin "Duke" Snider *Dodger centerfielder*
KID HARLEM   Marvin Jenkins *fighter*
THE HARLEM SPIDER   Tommy "Spider" Kelly *first bantamweight champ 1887*
THE BLACK EAGLE OF HARLEM   Col. Hubert F. Julian *mercenary*
THE STATEN ISLAND SCOT   Bobby Thomson *baseball player*
THE BAREFOOT BOY OF WALL STREET   Wendell Willkie *industrialist, politician*
THE WITCH OF WALL STREET   Hetty Green *financier*
BUFFALO BOB   Bob Smith *host of the TV show "Howdy Doody"*
THE BUFFALO HANGMAN, THE BUFFALO SHERIFF   (see Grover Cleveland, U.S.
   Presidents)
OLD KINDERHOOK   (see "Little Van" Matty Van Buren, U.S. Presidents)
ROCHESTER   (Eddie Anderson) *actor, Jack Benny's sidekick*

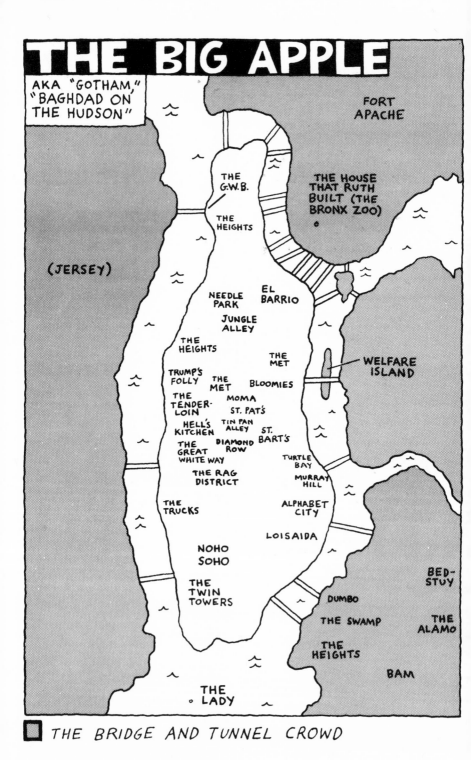

Smile When You Call Me That Department

THE WEST

THE COWBOY   Leland Verain "Two Gun" Alterie *gangster*
COWBOY   Lloyd E. Copas *country singer* / Jack Wills *fighter*
THE SINGING COWBOY, KING OF THE COWBOYS   Roy Rogers (Leonard Slye) *actor*
QUEEN OF THE COWGIRLS   Dale Evans (Frances Smith) *Leonard's wife*
AMERICA'S FAVORITE COWBOY   Tom Mix *actor*
THE ARIZONA COWBOY   Rex Allen *western star*
OKLAHOMA'S YODELING COWBOY   Gene Autry *actor, singer, entrepreneur*
THE COWBOY PHILOSOPHER, THE CHEROKEE KID   Will Rogers *humorist*
THE COWBOY SENATOR   Henry F. Ashurst *Arizona politician*
OLD PARD   Noble "Win" Ballou *baseball player*
THE DUDE   (see Chet Arthur, U.S. Presidents)
REDSKIN   Raleigh Aitchison *pitcher*
INDIAN   Jack Jacobs *Canadian football star*
THE OLD INDIAN   Early "Gus" Wynn *pitcher*
INDIAN BOB   Robert "Cherokee" Johnson *baseball player*
CHEROKEE BILL   William Hastings *Oklahoma politician*
CHIEF   Charles Bender *Indian pitcher* / Arnel Hale *baseball player*
BIG CHIEF   Charles Curtis *veep* / William S. Devery *NY police captain, 1900* / Russel Moore *trombonist* / William "God Knows" Taft (see U.S. Presidents)
THE GREAT WHITE CHIEF   (see Teddy Roosevelt, U.S. Presidents)
SUPERCHIEF   Allie Reynolds *pitcher*
CACTUS JACK   Garner (see "Poker Face," Head to Toe [Faces])
BEAR TRACKS   Al Javery, John Schmitz *baseball players*
THE IRON HORSE   Lou Gehrig (see "The Durable Dutchman," Them)
DEATH VALLEY JIM   James Scott *pitcher*
HOWDY   Howard Quicksell *banjo player* / Howard Wilcox II *car racer*

I Can't Face the Place, But the Name Is Familiar Department

THEM

Of all eloquence a nickname is the most concise and irresistible. It is a terse, pointed shorthand made of reasoning, condensing a volume of meaning into an epithet.

—William Mathews
Words: Their Use and Abuse 1876

HYMIE THE POLACK   Earl Wajcieckowski *bootlegger, aka "Father of the One-Way Ride"*

CHINK   Martin Abraham *bassist* / Earl Yingling *pitcher 1911–18*

DAGO   Frank Ciroficci *hitman circa 1910, died in "the chair" ("Old Smokey")*

THE LITTLE WOP   Oscar Melillo *infielder, aka "Ski," "Spinach"*

THE SCOTCH WOP   Johnny Dundee (Joseph Corrara) *junior lightweight champ 1921–23, featherweight champ 1923–24*

THE NAZI NAILER   Max "Mauling Maxie" Schmeling *German-born heavyweight champ 1930–32, aka "The Black Uhlan"*

JAP   Jasper Allen *tuba player*

THE MICK   Mickey Mantle *baseball great, aka "The Commerce Comet"*

THE MAD HUNGARIAN   Al Hrabosky *baseball player*

THE NERVOUS GREEK   Lou Skizas *baseball player*

THE TERRIBLE TURK   Thomas B. "Czar" Reed *Speaker of the House, aka "Biddy"*

THE ARGENTINE FIRECRACKER   Fanne Foxe *stripper, aka "The Tidal Basin Bombshell"*

THE BRAZILIAN BOMBSHELL   Carmen "The Chicka Boom-Boom Girl" Miranda *actress*

THE CUBAN BON BON   "Kid Chocolate" (Seligio Sardinias) *fighter*

THE DURABLE DANE   Battling Nelson (Oscar Neilson) *fighter*

THE DURABLE DUTCHMAN, COLUMBIA LOU   Lou Gehrig *baseball great, aka "The Iron Horse," "Larrupin' Lou," "Old Biscuit Pants"*

THE FLYING DUTCHMAN   John "Honus" Wagner *baseball Hall of Famer*

THE DUTCHMAN   Norm Van Brocklin *NFL quarterback*

DUTCH   (see Ron Reagan, U.S. Presidents)

DUTCH SCHULTZ   (Arthur Flegenheimer) *criminal*

BIG FINN   Lou Fiene *pitcher*

THE FLYING FINN   Paavo Nurmi *track star*

FRENCHY   Stanley Bordagaray *baseball player*

THE FLYING FRENCHMAN   *the Montreal Canadiens hockey team*

JIMMY THE GREEK   Jimmy Snyder *TV oddsmaker*

NICK THE GREEK   Nicholas Zographos *gambler*

THE GOLDEN GREEK   Harry Agganis *football player*

EL GRECO   (Domenikos Theotokopoulos) *Cretan artist in Spain*

GYPSY ROSE LEE   (Rose Louise Hovick) *stripper*

THE MEXICAN SPITFIRE   Lupe Velez *movie actress*

THE PULVERIZING POLE   Jadwiga Jedryejowska *tennis player*

THE SILENT POLE, THE GIANT KILLER   Harry Coveleski *pitcher*

THE FLYING SCOTSMAN   Jackie Stewart *car racer*

THE SILVER SCOT   Tommy Armour *golfer*

BIG SERB   Johnny Miljus *baseball player*

SHANGHAI BILL   (see "Wild Bill," Attitudes)

TOKYO ROSE (Iva Ikuko Toguri D'Aquino) *siren*
THE VAST VENETIAN (see "The Ambling Alp," Movement)
MOONMAN Mike Shannon *baseball player*

"Call Me a Cab" "All Right, You're a Cab" Department

GETTING THERE

CAB Cabell Calloway *bandleader* / Don Kolloway *baseball player, aka "Butch"*
HACK Lewis Wilson *baseball Hall of Famer, aka "The Million Dollar Baby from the 5 & 10 Cent Store"*
CADILLAC William Smith *NY politician* / Nelson Williams *trumpet player*
HOT ROD Rod Gilbert *hockey player* / Rod Hundley, John Williams *basketball players*
WHEELS Frank "Tex" Carswell *baseball player*
TRUCK Charles Parham *bassist*
FIRE TRUCKS Virgil Trucks *relief pitcher*
BUS Emile Mossbacker, Jr. *football player*
JEEP Lee Handley, Don Heffner *baseball players*
SCOOTER Phil Rizzuto *baseball player, announcer*
SPARKPLUG Jim Keenan *pitcher*
HORSEPOWER Hampton Pitts Fulmer *politician*
KING OF THE ROAD Roger Miller *singer, songwriter*
THE COLOSSUS OF ROADS Edward H. Harriman, John L. McAdam *financiers*
SPEED DEMON Pasquale Agati *car racer*
ROADBLOCK Sherman Jones *baseball player*
CRASH Billy Craddock *rock singer*
FATHER OF THE ONE-WAY RIDE Earl Wajcieckowski *bootlegger, aka "Hymie the Polack"*
TRACTOR Bill Lesuk *hockey player*
WAGON TONGUE (see Head to Toe [Mouths])
TANK, MINI TANK, BATTLESHIP, GUNBOAT, SUB, THE MEXICAN SPITFIRE (see Weapons)
TROLLEY LINE Johnny Butler *baseball player*
TRAM Frankie Trumbauer *trumpet player*
THE SUBWAY VIGILANTE Bernhard Goetz *(shot 4 alleged muggers in 1984)*
'TRANE John Coltrane *sax great*
BIG TRAIN Walter "Barney" Johnson *baseball great*
LITTLE TRAIN Lionel James *football player*
NIGHT TRAIN Richard Lane *football player*
RUNAWAY TRAIN Preben Elkjaer *soccer player*
TRAINWRECK Tom Novack *All-American Cornhusker*
THE LINCOLN LOCOMOTIVE Leo Lewis *football player*

THE LITTLE STEAM ENGINE   James "Pud" Galvin *baseball player*
CHOO-CHOO   Charlie Brown *fighter* / Clarence Coleman *original Met* / Charlie Justice *football player*
THE IRON HORSE   Lou Gehrig (see "Durable Dutchman," Them)
THE EBONY EXPRESS   Jesse Owens *Olympic track star, aka "The Ebony Antelope"*
THE FARGO EXPRESS   Billy Petrolle *fighter*
THE SINGING BRAKEMAN   Jimmy Rogers *country music great*
CHET THE JET   Chester Walker *basketball player*
THE GOLDEN JET   Bobby Hull *hockey player*
THE GLIDER   Ed Charles *baseball player*
AIRPLANE EARS   John Z. Anderson *politician*
FLIGHT 45   Dave Smith *baseball player*
THE SENATOR FROM BOEING   Henry "Scoop" Jackson *Washington politician*
AIRMAIL   William H. Morton *football player*
THE BLIMP   Ernest G. Phelps *politician*
THE WILD HELICOPTER   Edgar Jones *basketball player*
THE ROCKET   Rod Foster *basketball player*
ROCKET   Maurice Richard *hockey player*
THE POCKET ROCKET   (see Love & Sex)
STEAMBOAT   Clem Dreisewerd, Rees Williams *baseball players*
RIVERBOAT   Robert Smith *pitcher*
SHOWBOAT   George Fisher *baseball player*
TUG   Frank McGraw *pitcher*
SCOW   Fay Thomas *baseball player*
THE CRUISER   Julio Cruz *baseball player*
THE CHINA CLIPPER   Normie Kwong *Canadian football player*
THE YANKEE CLIPPER   (see "Joltin' Joe," Assorted Mayhem)
THE MAYFLOWER MADAM   Sydney Biddle Barrows *blueblood, former madam*
THE FLYING DUTCHMAN   John "Honus" Wagner *baseball Hall of Famer*
TITANIC   Alvin Clarence Thompson *gambler*
ICEBERG   (see Benjamin Harrison, U.S. Presidents)
THE UNSINKABLE MOLLY BROWN   Margaret Tobin Brown *Titanic survivor*
THE CAPSIZE KID   Ted Turner *financier, sailor, aka "Captain Outrageous"*
SHIPWRECK   Alvin A. Kelly *flagpole sitter*
JOE CARGO   Joe Valachi *criminal*
JUNKET JERRY   Gerals P. Nye *isolationist North Dakota senator*
THE LITTLE GLOBETROTTER   Billy Earle *baseball player*
COMMUTER RALPH   Ralph Lumenti *baseball player*
HIKER   Albert Moran *pitcher*
JUDY HOLLIDAY   (Judith Tuvim) *actress*
SUITCASE   Sam Johnson *singer* / Robert Seeds, Harry Simpson *baseball players*
BAGS   Milton "Milt" Jackson *musician*

SATCHELL   Leroy Paige *pitcher*
SATCHMO (SATCHELL MOUTH)   (see Head to Toe [Mouths])
KIT   Christopher Carson *frontier scout*

Rattlers Department

RAILROAD LINES

Just busted out? On the bum? Thinking about jumping a string of flats? Before you catch a getaway, you'll need to know a few tramp nicknames for railway lines. These were popular among the brotherhood in the dirty '30s:

APPLE BUTTER ROUTE   the N&W
BEEFSTEAK AND ONIONS; THE DOPE   the Baltimore & Ohio
BUMPY, ROCKY, AND PECULIAR; BERP   the BR&P
BIG SUITCASE   the Grand Trunk Line
BITTER BISCUIT LINE   the Piedmont section of the Southern
CARRY-ALL   the Chicago & Alton
CASEY   the Kansas City Southern
COLD, HUNGRY, AND DIRTY; COLD, HUNGRY, AND DRY   the CH&D
COME IN AND WAIT   the CI&W
COUGH AND SNORT   the Colorado & Southern
DELAY AND HESITATE   the D&H
DOUGHNUT LANE   the Pennsylvania, Trenton to Harrisburg
EMPTY CARS AND NO RAILROAD   the EC&N
EXCESS TONNAGE AND SLOW FREIGHT   the Atchison, Topeka & Sante Fe
GILA MONSTER ROUTE   the Southern Pacific, Maricopa to Yuma
HOBO AND TIN CAN ROUTE   the Houston & Texas Central
IRISH RAILROAD; Q   the Chicago, Burlington & Quincy
KATY LINES   the Missouri, Kansas & Texas lines
LEAVE EARLY AND WALK   the LE&W
LESS SLEEP AND MORE SPEED   the Lake Shore & Michigan Southern
MAY LUNGE AND TURN OVER   the ML&T
MISERY PACIFIC; MOP   the Missouri Pacific
MODEL T   the DT&I
MUDDLE AND GET NOWHERE   the Midland & Great Northern
OLD AND WEARY; OLD WOMAN   the New York, Ontario & Western
ONION ROUTE   the Chicago & Wabash Valley
SNAKY   the Oregon & California
SOUP LINE   the Southern Pacific
SPUD DRAG   the Bangor & Aroostook
TIRED, POOR, AND WEARY   the Toledo, Peoria & Western
WHISKEY CENTRAL   the Wisconsin Central

We Call It Corn, But They Call It Maize Department
or,
The Masked Man I Know, But Did You Catch His Faithful Indian Companion's Name?

INDIANS

The various tribes of native North Americans had various ways of getting and giving personal names—often an individual had several. Children were frequently given "apatropic" names, ugly nasty ones, so that evil spirits would avoid them. Of these, Turtle Anus was an especial favorite.

Sometimes a young brave went on a "name hunt," to search for the "vision" which would give him his name; this is the way "Crazy Horse" (Tashunka Witco) found his name; and another Sioux warrior, originally called, unflatteringly, Hunkesni, that is, "Slow," changed his name after his vision and became Yotanka, "Sitting Bull."

A notable adult achievement could earn you another name: The Sioux leader "Morning Star" defeated an enemy in hand to hand combat armed only with a dull knife, and was called "Dull Knife" thereafter.

The new European arrivals gave the "Indians" new names: "King Philip," the settlers called the first red man to fight back. He was Wagwises, "Circling Fox," and Metacom, "Chief's House" to the Wampanoag people.

The whites with whom he refused to make peace called the Seminole leader of the early 1800s "Billy Bowlegs." He was truly Holata Micco, "Alligator Chief."

Sometimes the Europeans were generous enough to "christen" the savages, that is, give them "christian names" . . . you know, *saints'* names. The Apache warrior Goyathly ("The Yawner") was called, by the Spanish missionaries, after St. Jerome. To them and us he became Geronimo. The Navajo chieftain known to his people as "Holy Boy" and "Man of the Black Weeds," whose war name was "Angry Warrior," was just Manuelito—"Little Manuel"—to the settlers. The Kawai (California) leader baptized Juan Antonio was Cooswootna Yampoochee, "He Who Gets Angry Quickly."

The most famous "Indian" of recent times we know by his paleface name, Jim Thorpe. The great athlete's Sac-Fox "real" name was Wathohuck, "Bright Path."

The Indian on the "buffalo" nickel, or at least the model for that noble profile, was (until his death in 1934) widely known by the romantic title "John Two Guns White Calf": a name he was given by the public relations department of the Great Northern Railway.

6

THE NAMES
OF THE GAME

I even had a nickname. You have to have a nickname to be remembered.
—Hero of the 1954 World Series for the Giants James Lamar "Dusty"
Rhodes (now working as a cook on a tugboat), quoted in
Where Have You Gone, Vince DiMaggio?

BASEBALL'S HALL OF NAME

In Phillip Roth's *The Great American Novel,* a rookie ballplayer named
Damur becomes obsessed with his need for a nickname. He beseeches his
teammates to call him "Babe," "Stretch," "Bonehead," "Highpockets"—
but none of the traditional monikers fits. Eventually, he takes the field,
announced as "Nickname Damur."

*Sweetbreads Bailey, Desperate Beatty, The Darling Booth, Buttermilk
Tommy Dowd, Leaky Faucett, Herky Jerky Horton, Hippety Hopp, Sugar
Kane, Earache Meyer, Spooks Speake, Silk Stocking Schaeffer, Peekaboo
Veach . . .*

Is the baseball nickname an endangered species? *The New York Times*
said as much in midsummer 1986. Why? The *Times* reporter placed the
blame on "soaring salaries, mass electronic media . . . and today's players'
image for advertising." (While he was at it, he might have blamed artificial
turf, the graduated income tax, and junk food.)

Yet the New York Mets, who dominated the '86 season, was a team of
old-fashioned nicknames: pitchers Dwight "Doctor K" Gooden, Sid "El
Sid," "Squidly" Fernandez, and reliever Roger "Skeeter" McDowell . . .
catcher Gary "The Kid" Carter, Keith "Quiche," "Mex" Hernandez at first
base, Wally "Cabbage Patch" Backman at second, Kevin "World" Mitchell

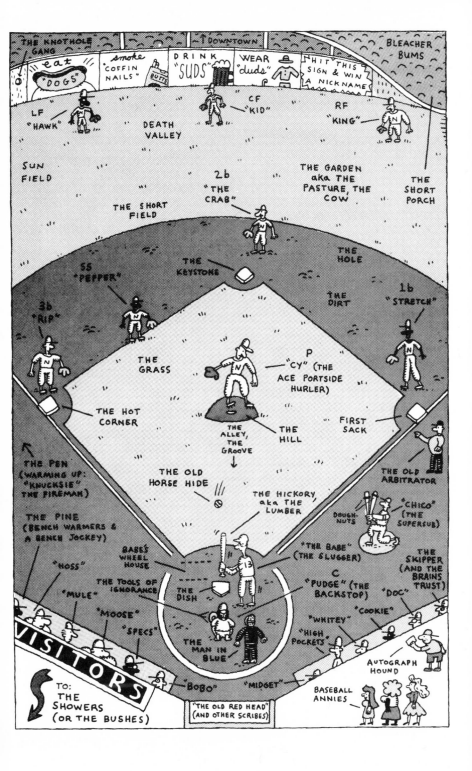

at short, Howard "Hojo" Johnson at third, and an outfield of Lee "The Italian Stallion" Mazzilli, William Howard "Mookie" Wilson, and Lennie "Nails" Dykstra.

One hundred and seventy-eight former major leaguers have been elected to Baseball's Hall of Fame in Cooperstown, New York. One hundred and sixty-five of them were "famous long ago" by their nicknames.

As might be expected, these monikers are of all types: insulting, like "Fat Kid" Killibrew and "Kiki" Cuyler (he stuttered) . . . by geographical origin—"The Georgia Peach" Ty Cobb, "The Duke of Tralee" Roger Bresnahan . . . descriptive, as in "Mechanical Man" Charlie Gehringer, or "Mr. Sunshine" Ernie Banks . . . "inevitable," such as "Stonewall" (Travis) Jackson and "Hoot" (Bob) Gibson . . . and often of the flowery-epithet variety concocted by sportswriters, e.g., "The Peerless Leader" Frank Chance and "The Man with the Golden Arm" Sandy Koufax. (One hardly imagines a teammate shouting to Herb Pennock, "Hey! Save me a lick, Knight of Kennet Square!")

As with all things baseball-related, George Herman Ruth serves as the exemplar. To would-be-poetic columnists, he was "The Bambino" and "The Sultan of Swat." To his Yankee teammates, he was "Jidge." The kids back in the orphanage had called him "Nig," which racial epithet remained popular with opposing team "bench jockeys." He called himself "The Baby." His plaque in Cooperstown says "Babe."

Here are his fellow immortals, nickname by nickname:

Cobb, Tyrus R., "Ty," "The Georgia Peach," "The Idol of Baseball Fandom"
Wagner, John P., "Honus," "The Flying Dutchman," "Hans"
Ruth, George Herman, "Babe," "The Sultan of Swat," "The Bambino," "Jidge"
Mathewson, Christopher, "Christy," "Big Six," "Matty the Great"
Johnson, Walter, "Barney," "The Big Train," "Swede"
Lajoie, Napoleon, "Nap," "Larry," "King Larry"
Speaker, Tristram, "Tris," "Spoke," "The Grey Eagle"
McGillicuddy, Cornelius, "Connie Mack," "The Tall Tactician"
McGraw, John, "Muggsy," "Little Napoleon"
Alexander, Grover Cleveland, "Ol' Pete"
Sisler, George, "Gorgeous George," "The Perfect Ballplayer," "The Brown Blaster"
Collins, Edward, "Cocky"
Keeler, William, "Wee Willie," "Hit 'Em Where They Ain't"
Gehrig, H. Louis, "Laruppin' Lou," "Columbia Lou," "The Iron Horse," "The Durable Dutchman," "Old Biscuit Pants"
Anson, Adrian, "Cap," "Infant," "Pop"
Comiskey, Charles, "Commy," "The Old Roman"

Cummings, William, "Candy," "The Father of the Curveball"
Ewing, William, "Buck"
Radbourne, Charles, "Ol' Hoss"
Hornsby, Rogers, "Rajah"
Bresnahan, Roger, "The Duke of Tralee"
Brouthers, Dennis, "Big Dan"
Clarke, Fred, "Cap"
Delahanty, Edward, "Big Ed," "The Only Del"
Duffy, Hugh, "Duffmeier"
Jennings, Hughie, "Eee-Yah"
Kelly, Michael, "King," "The $10,000 Beauty"
O'Rouke, James, "Orator Jim"
Robinson, Wilbert, "Grapefruit," "Uncle Robbie"
Burkett, Jesse, "The Crab"
Chance, Frank, "Husk," "The Peerless Leader"
Chesbro, John, "Happy Jack"
Evers, Johnny, "The Crab," "The Trojan"
Griffith, Clarke, "The Old Fox"
McCarthy, Tommy, "The Heavenly Twins" (with Hugh Duffy)
McGinnity, Joseph, "Iron Man"
Plank, Edward, "Gettysburg Eddie"
Waddell, George, "Rube"
Walsh, Edward, "Big Ed," "Big Moose"
Hubbell, Carl, "The Meal Ticket," "King Carl," "Old Soupbone," "The Meek Man
    from Meeker," "The Meeker Magician"
Frisch, Frankie, "The Fordham Flash"
Cochrane, Gordon, "Mickey," "Black Mike"
Grove, Robert, "Lefty," "Mose," "Lightning"
Pennock, Herb, "The Squire of Kennet Square"
Traynor, Harold J., "Pie"
Gehringer, Charlie, "The Mechanical Man," "The Fowlerville Flailer"
Averill, Earl, "The Rock," "The Earl of Snohomish"
Harris, Stanley, "Bucky," "The Boy Wonder"
Herman, William Jennings, "Bryan"
Johnson, William, "Judy," "Sweet Juice"
Roberts, Robert, "Robin"
Lemon, Bob, "Lem"
Connor, Roger, "Dear Old Roger"
Lindstrom, Freddie, "Lindy"
Charleston, Oscar, "Charlie," "The Hoosier Comet"
Banks, Ernie, "Mr. Cub," "Mr. Sunshine"
Russie, Amos, "The Hoosier Thunderbolt"
Lopez, Al, "El Señor"

Lloyd, John Henry, "Pop," "Cuchara"
DiHigo, Martin, "El Maestro"
Mathews, Eddie, "Eddy Mattress"
Joss, Adrian, "Addie"
Mays, Willie, "The Say Hey Kid," "Amazing Mays"
Wilson, Lewis, "Hack," "The Million Dollar Baby from the 5 & 10 Cent Store"
Snider, Edwin, "Duke," "The Silver Fox," "The Duke of Flatbush"
Klein, Chuck, "The Hoosier Hammerer"
Gibson, Bob, "Hoot," "The Old Master"
Mize, Johnny, "Big Cat"
Foster, Andrew, "Rube"
Aaron, Henry, "Bad Henry," "The Hammer"
Robinson, Frank, "Robby"
Jackson, Travis, "Stonewall," "The Arkansas Traveler"
Combs, Earle, "The Kentucky Colonel," "The Mail Carrier"
Haines, Jesse, "Pop"
Bancroft, Dave, "Beauty"
Beckley, Jake, "Eagle Eye," "Blitzer"
Hafey, Charles, "Chick"
Kelley, Joseph, "Honest Joe"
Marquand, Richard, "Rube"
Paige, Leroy, "Satchel"
Koufax, Sanford, "Sandy," "Koo," "The Man with the Golden Arm"
Berra, Lawrence Peter, "Yogi"
Wynn, Early, "Gus," "The Old Indian"
Gomez, Vernon, "Lefty," "Goofy"
Youngs, Ross, "Pep"
Gibson, Josh, "The Black Babe Ruth"
Leonard, Walter Fenner, "Buck"
Spahn, Warren, "Spahnie," "The Invincible One"
Kelly, George, "Highpockets," "Long George"
Welch, Michael, "Smiling Mickey"
Irvin, Monford, "Monte"
Clemente, Roberto, "Arriba," "Bob," "The Great One"
Mantle, Mickey, "The Mick," "The Commerce Comet"
Ford, Edward, "Whitey," "The Chairman of the Board"
Bottomley, James, "Sunny Jim"
Conlan, John, "Jocko"
Thompson, Samuel, "Big Sam"
Bell, James, "Cool Papa"
Kiner, Ralph, "Mr. Home Run"
Brown, Mordecai, "Three Finger," "Miner"
Nichols, Charles, "Kid"

Ott, Mel, "Master Melvin"
Foxx, Jimmy, "Double X," "The Beast"
Heilmann, Harry, "Slug"
Waner, Paul, "Big Poison," "Oakie"
Dean, Jay H., "Dizzy"
Simmons, Al, "Bucketfoot," "The Duke of Milwaukee"
Bender, Charles, "Chief"
Wallace, Roderick, "Rhody," "Bobby"
Maranville, Walter J., "Rabbit"
Dickey, Bill, "Baseball's Quiet Man"
Terry, William, "Memphis Bill"
DiMaggio, Joseph, "The Yankee Clipper," "Joltin' Joe," "Joe D."
Lyons, Ted, "The Sunday Pitcher"
Vance, Clarence, "Dazzy"
Hartnett, Charles, "Gabby," "Old Tomato Face"
Baker, John Franklin, "Home Run," "Frank"
Schalk, Ray, "Cracker"
Greenberg, Henry, "Hammerin' Hank"
Cronin, Joe, "Mr. Clutch"
Crawford, Samuel, "Wahoo Sam," "The Wahoo Barber"
McCarthy, Joseph, "Marse Joe"
Wheat, Zack, "Buck"
Carey, Max, "Scoops"
Hamilton, William, "Sliding Billy"
Feller, Bob, "Rapid Robert," "Bullet Bob"
Robinson, Jackie, "Black Jack," "The First"
McKechnie, Bill, "Deacon"
Rice, Edgar Charles, "Sam"
Rixey, Jephtha, "Eppa Jeptha"
Appling, Luke, "Old Aches and Pains"
Faber, Uran C., "Red"
Grimes, Burleigh, "Ol' Stubblebeard," "Boilin' Boily," "The Senator," "The Last of
    the Spitball Pitchers"
Huggins, Miller, "Hug," "Flea," "The Mighty Mite"
Keefe, Tim, "Sir Timothy"
Manush, Henry, "Heinie"
Ward, John Montgomery, "Monte"
Galvin, James, "Pud," "The Little Steam Engine"
Williams, Theodore, "Teddy Ballgame," "The Thumper," "The Kid," "The Splendid
    Splinter"
Stengel, Charles Dillon, "Casey," "The Old Perfesser"
Ruffing, Charles, "Red"
Rickey, Wesley Branch, "The Mahatma"

Waner, Lloyd, "Little Poison"
Medwick, Joe, "Ducky Wucky," "Muscles," "Mickey"
Cuyler, Hazen Shirley, "Kiki," "Cuy"
Goslin, Leon, "Goose"
Musial, Stanley Frank, "Stan the Man"
Campanella, Roy, "Campy"
Coveleski, Harry, "The Silent Pole," "The Giant Killer"
Hoyt, Waite, "Schoolboy"
Boudreau, Lou, "The Boy Manager"
Robinson, Brooks, "Mr. Impossible," "The Hoover," "The Human Vacuum Cleaner"
Marichal, Juan, "Manito," "The Dominican Dandy"
Keller, Charlie, "King Kong"
Aparicio, Luis, "Little Louie"
Killibrew, Harmon, "Killer," "The Fat Kid"
Drysdale, Don, "Double D"
Reese, Harold, "Pee Wee," "The Little Colonel"
Wilhelm, Hoyt, "Old Sarge"
Brock, Lou, "The Base Burglar"
Slaughter, Enos, "Country"
Vaughan, Joseph, "Arky"
McCovey, Willie, "Stretch"
Lombardi, Ernie, "Schnozz," "Bocci"
Williams, Billy, "Sweet Swingin' "
Hunter, Jim, "Catfish"

You Can't Tell the Players Without a Nickname Department

GRIDIRON MONIKERS

There are nearly five thousand major league baseball games a season, and as few as eighteen men appear in each. There are fewer than two hundred pro football games a year, and as many as eighty players take part in every contest. Baseball players stand (or run) around barefaced, wearing flimsy pajamas. Football players swarm, encased in masks and armor. Baseball players nearly all acquire nicknames. Only the rare footballer earns a term of endearment. William "The Refrigerator" Perry of the Chicago Bears is a recent example—a figure so delightfully preposterous, with a tag so felicitous, playing for a championship team.

The original football superstar was Harold "Red" Grange, "The Galloping Ghost." Another early spectacular open-field runner was Elroy "Crazy

Legs" Hirsch. Appropriately named power backs have been (Hall of Famers) Dick "Night Train" Lane, Earle "Greasy" Neale, Alan "The Horse" Ameche, "Johnny Blood" McNally, and O. J. "Juice" Simpson.

Quarterbacks and kickers who perform "solo" (like baseball players) are more likely to acquire sobriquets: "Sir" Francis Tarkenton, aka "Fran the Scrambler" . . . "Slingin' " Sammy Baugh . . . Roger "The Dodger" Staubach . . . Lou "The Toe" Groza . . . and "Automatic" Ben Agajanian.

Even some linemen and/or defensive players achieve the stature of a nickname: "Mean" Joe Green, "Big Daddy" Lipscombe, "Too Tall" Jones, Alex "The Mad Duck" Karras, and "The Assassin" Jack Tatum.

And a penchant for off-the-field eccentricity sometimes helps: "Broadway Joe" Namath, Paul "Golden Boy" Hornung, Kenny "Snake" Stabler,

Thomas "Hollywood" Henderson, and "Whiskey" Billy Kilmer all made headlines in their time, not necessarily on the sports pages.

They're the guys who get to do the commercials.

Occasionally, a group of baseball players are nicknamed as a group: "The Gashouse Gang," "Murderer's Row," "The Million Dollar Infield" . . . but in football the practice is much more common.

Blame it on sportswriter Grantland "Granny" Rice, who dubbed the Fordham line "The Seven Blocks of Granite," and the Notre Dame backfield of Miller, Hayden, Crowley, and Stuhldreher "The Four Horsemen of the Apocalypse." LA's defensive line was once "The Fearsome Foursome," Pittsburg's "The Steel Curtain," Minnesota's "The Purple People Eaters," Denver's "The Orange Crush."

Let's Just Call Him the Golden Golden! Department

NICKNAMES ON ICE

Are Canadians naturally unimaginative? A hockey play-by-play announcer, watching Boston's magnificent defenseman Bobby Orr execute an end-to-end rush, once shrieked into his mike, "Jeez! If they call Bobby Hull 'The Golden Jet,' what can we call Orr? 'The Golden *Golden*'?!!!"

Hull was a (balding) blond Chicago forward whose "Golden Jet" tag so tickled hockey fans that when he joined the Winnipeg team, its name was changed to "Jets." In truth, Hull's sobriquet was merely a change rung on the nickname of the aptly dubbed (he was both fast and explosive) Maurice "The Rocket" Richard, of the Montreal Canadiens.

Get a load of these spectacularly original nicknames adorning the members of hockey's Hall of Fame: "Ace," "Babe," "Butch," "Cat," "Chief," "Dutch," "Duke," "Hap," "King," "Moose," "Red," "Shorty," "Tiny" . . .

Not one of the game's true superstars, Howie Morenz, Gordie Howe, or Bobby Orr, had a nickname (unless you count "Golden Golden," I guess); and the best they can do for the best player in history, Edmonton's Wayne Gretsky, is "The Great."

There are, of course, exceptions. Scoring threat Nels Stewart was "Old Poison," slap-shotting Bernie Geffrion was "Boom-Boom" (for the sound of six-yard-wide-of-the-net blasts echoing off the boards), and Maurice Richard's little brother Henri, a star in his own right, was "The Pocket Rocket."

Like football players, perhaps, hockey players earn interesting nicknames in *groups:* "The Broad Street Bullies" was perfect for the aggressive

Philadelphia Flyer teams of the '70s, and the Canadiens' fast and freewheeling style has earned them their "Flying Frenchmen" handle.

Scoring combinations, as well, have received some interesting titles over the years: the Canadiens' combo of Richard, Elmer Lach, and Hector "Toe" Blake was "The Punch Line" . . . Boston's "Kraut Line" was made up of Milt Schmidt, Woody Dumart, and Bobby Baur . . . Toronto's "Kid Line" matched rookies Joe Primeau, Joe "Busher" Jackson, and Charlie "Bomber" Conacher . . . Gordie Howe played alongside "Terrible" Ted Lindsey and Sid "Bootnose" Abel for Detroit on "The Production Line" . . . and recently Buffalo combined Gil Perreault, Rick Martin, and Rene Robert to form "The French Connection."

Hockey goaltenders are loners. Flakes. Individuals. They stand out— and they get nicknames as a consequence. Shutout artist Frankie Brimseck was "Mr. Zero." Frequently sprawling Jim Walsh was "Flat." Don Simmons of Boston was "Dippy," Lorne Worsley (the last goalie to play without a mask) was "Gump," and Jacques Plante (the first to wear a mask) was "Jake the Snake." Gary Smith played for ten teams in ten years—"Suitcase," he was called. The Toronto Maple Leafs' nets have been guarded by Walter "Turk" Broda, Harry "Applecheeks" Lumley, "Ageless" Johnny Bower, aka "The China Wall," and Mike Palmateer, "The Popcorn Kid."

Roundball, Hoops, the City Game Department

BASKETBALL

Ten men in their underwear running and jumping around a small floor in full view of thousands—ideal conditions for the spontaneous generation of nicknames. Yet, until somebody got the bright idea that maybe black men could play the game, too, basketball history hardly provided a cornucopia of spectacular tags. From the Hall of Fame:

John "Becky" Beckman, "The Babe Ruth of Basketball"
"Poison" Joe Brennan
Henry "Dutch" Dehnert
Harold "Bud" Foster
"Jumping" Joe Fulks
Edward "Moose" Krause
"Foothills" Bobo Kurland
"Jumping" Jack McCracken
"Easy" Ed Macauley

Charles "Stretch" Murphy
Jim Pollard, "The Kangaroo Kid"
Adolph "Dolph" Schayes
Ernest "One Grand" Shmidt
John "Cat" Thompson
John Wooden, "The India Rubber Man"

Then, in 1950, the Celtics started Ed "Chuck" Cooper and the Knicks hired Nat "Sweetwater" Clifton away from the Globetrotters, and soon the game was adorned by superstars with nicknames as startling and brilliant as graffiti on a playground wall . . .

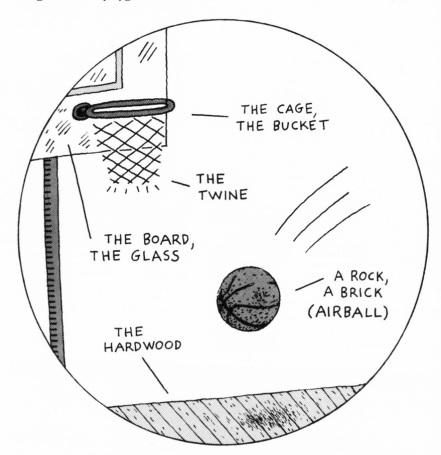

Nate "Tiny" Archibald, aka "Nate the Skate"
"Dollar" Bill Bradley
Wilt Chamberlain, "The Stilt" to the media, but self-named "The Big Dipper"
Charles "Tarzan" Cooper
Clyde "The Glide" Drexler
Daryl Dawkins, "Earthquake," aka "Chocolate Thunder"
Julius Erving, "Dr. J."
Walt Frazier, known as "Clyde" for his ball-banditry
"The Mad Bomber" Richard Fuqun
Lloyd "World Be" Free
"Daddy Hooves" Gus Gerrard
Darrel Griffith, "Doctor Dunkenstein"
John "Hondo" Havlicek
Earvin "Magic" Johnson
Edgar Jones, "The Wild Helicopter"
"Pistol Pete" Maravich
Earl "The Pearl" Monroe
Akeem "The Dream" Olajuwun
Chet "The Jet" Walker
Dominique Wilkins, "The Human Highlight Film"

Moments of Truth Department

BULLFIGHTING

Bullfighting, another "one-man" sport, is, however, nickname heaven. *Every* matador has a sobriquet. Many of them are place names—origin nicknames: for example, the celebrated "El Cordobes," Manuel Benitez, was born in Cordoba. Some are diminutives: "Joselito" was Jose Ortega Gomez. But many are terse, poetic descriptions of style:

Vincente Bernabe, "El Caracol" ("The Snail")
Juan Cabello, "El Brujo" ("The Wizard")
Antonio de la Haba, "Zurito" ("Little Wild Dove")
Antonio Escobar y Mellado, "El Boto" ("The Bore")
Alfred Gomez, "El Brillanto" ("The Shining Little One")
José Gomez, "El Alba" ("The Dawn")
Raphael Gomez Ortega, "El Divino Calvo" ("The Divine Baldy")
Julio Gomez y Canete, "Relampaguito" ("Little Lightning Flash")
Andrez Jimenez Torres, "El Monaguillo" ("The Altar Boy")
Tomas Parrondo, "El Manchado" ("The Spotted One")

Titleholders Department

BOXING

Which brings us to the most "personal" sport of all: boxing. Two individuals, nearly naked, fighting for fame, glory, money, survival, on a brightly lit stage, before a partisan and (to a remarkable extent) knowledgeable crowd. Boxing fans identify with their fighter, champ, or underdog. In the classic nickname tradition, his ring name connects him to a region ("The Dixie Kid," "Rocky Kansas"), to a neighborhood ("Harlem Tommy" Kelly, Ruby "The Pride of the Ghetto" Goldstein), to a hometown ("Philadelphia Jack" O'Brien, Rocky "The Brockton Bomber" Marciano), or to his ethnic origins (Joe "The Brown Bomber" Louis, "Irish Jack" Murphy).

Naturally, "totem" animals abound: "Tiger" Flowers, "Gorilla" Jones, Archie "The Mongoose" Moore . . . there are terms of high praise: "Nonpareil" Dempsey, "Stonehands" Duran . . . even insults: "Slapsie Maxie," "Two-Ton Tony," "The Bayonne Bleeder."

The first (bareknuckle) heavyweight champion of England, James Figg, lost his title to George "The Barber" Taylor in 1735, to begin a tradition of vocational nicknames: Billy "The Nailer" Stevens, George "The Collier" Meggs, George "The Baker" Millsom, Tom "The Water Man" Lyons.

In 1784, Jack Fearns, who fought under the assumed name of "Duggan," was defeated by Thomas "Jackling" (nee Johnson). He in turn lost to "Big Ben" Brain, who was defeated by the first Jewish champ, Daniel Mendoza, "The Light of Israel." Next came John "Gentleman Jack" Jackson, who retired from the ring to assume a seat in parliament.

James "Jem" Belcher, in 1805, was beaten by Henry Pearce—"Hen" for short, and thus "The Game Chicken."

In 1818, Tom Spring took the title—his ring name was "Tom Winter"; he was succeeded, in turn, by "The Great Gun of Windsor," Tom Cannon, then Jem "The Black Diamond" Ward.

James "Deaf" Burke, aka "The Deaf 'Un," wore the crown from 1828 to 1839, when it was assumed by William Thompson, who battled under the mysterious single pseudonym of "Bendingo," champion until 1850.

For the last thirty years of bareknuckle pugilism, the title was claimed by a variety of fighters, British and American, including William Perry, "The Tipton Slasher," Tom Sayers, "The Napoleon of the Prize Ring," and Jem "The Gypsy" Mace, who fought off all comers from 1866 to 1873.

Last of the bareknuckle and first of the gloved champions was John L. Sullivan, "The Boston Strong Boy." Here are his successors:

1892   James J. Corbett, "Gentleman Jim"
1897   Bob Fitzsimmons, "Ruby Robert"
1899   James J. Jeffries, "The Boilermaker," aka "The Beast"
1906   Tommy Burns (Noah Brusso), "Tahmy"
1908   Jack Johnson, "The Galveston Giant," aka "The Big Smoke," "Li'l Arthur"
1915   Jess Willard, "The Potawatomi Giant," aka "Cowboy Jess," "The Great
         White Hope"
1919   (William) Jack[1] Dempsey, "The Manassa Mauler," aka "The Giant Killer"
1926   Gene Tunney, "The Fighting Marine"
1930   Max Schmeling, "The Black Uhlan," aka "The Nazi Nailer"
1932   Jack Sharkey (Joseph Cukoschay), "The Boston Gob," aka "The Fighting
         Fool," "The Gabby Lithuanian"
1933   Primo Carnera, "The Ambling Alp," aka "Ponderous Primo," "The Preem"
1934   Max Baer,[2] "The Livermore Larruper," aka "Bearcat," "The California
         Muscleman," "Butcherboy," "Fighting Bear," "The Livermore Lover,"
         "Mad Max," "Madcap Maxie"
1935   James J. Braddock, "The Cinderella Man"
1937   Joe Louis (Barrow), "The Brown Bomber," aka "Alabam' Assassin," "Black
         Beauty," "Brown Behemoth," "Dark Destroyer," "Detroit's Dun Demon,"
         "The Licorice Lasher," "Michigan Mauler," "Ring Robot," "Sable
         Sphinx," "Sepia Sniper," "Tan Thunderbolt," "Wildcat Warrior"
1949   Ezzard Charles, "The Cincinnati Cobra"
1951   Joe Walcott (Arnold Cream),[3] "Jersey Joe"
1952   Rocky Marciano (Rocco Marchegiano), "The Brockton Blockbuster"
1956   Floyd Patterson, "The Rabbit"
1959   Ingemar Johansson
1962   Charles Liston, "Sonny," aka "The Big Ugly Bear"
1964   Muhammad Ali[4] (Cassius Clay), "The Louisville Lip," aka "The Mouth That
         Roared," "The Greatest"
1970   Joe Frazier, "Smokin' Joe"
1973   George Foreman, "Big George," aka "Monkey," "The Lightning Destroyer"
1978   Leon Spinks, "Neon Leon," aka "Mess-over"

   1. Dempsey borrowed the "Jack" from another Dempsey, a former middleweight title-
holder (1884–91) nicknamed, incidentally, "The Nonpareil." The earlier Dempsey's real name
was John Kelly.
   2. The number of sobriquets assigned to the undistinguished Max Baer in 1934 suggests
that nicknaming was a popular depression-era pastime; *vide* the plethora of tags hung on Joe
Louis, or, for that matter, Ruth, Gehrig, and FDR.
   3. Jersey Joe's real name was no secret; when Marciano trounced him for the title, the
Daily News headline read: WHIPPED CREAM.
   4. Ali (somewhat unfairly) dubbed Patterson "Rabbit," but with poetic justice called Liston
"The Big Ugly Bear."

7
YOU KNOW THE TYPE

Call Me Irresponsible Department

ATTITUDES

You jig, you amble, and you lisp, and nickname God's creatures . . . it hath made me mad.

—Prince Hamlet, "The Melancholy Dane"

SERIOUS   Wilson Myers *bassist*
GLOOMY GIL   Gilmore Dobie *football coach*
GLOOMY GUS[1]   (see "Tricky" Dick Nixon, U.S. Presidents)
SAD SAM   Samuel Jones *pitcher, aka "Toothpick"*
AGONY AL   Al Agett *football player*
DOUR DENNY   Denny Shute *golfer*
TERRIBLE-TEMPERED   Tommy Bolt *golfer*
BITTER   Ambrose Bierce *American satirist, author of* The Devil's Dictionary
GRUMP   Hal Irelan *baseball player*
GRUMPS   Mike Bragg *football player*
GROUCHO   Julius Marx *brother of "Harpo" (Adolph), "Chico" (Leonard), "Gummo" (Milton), and "Zeppo" (Herbert)*
CRABBY   Estel Crabtree *baseball player*
THE CRAB   Jesse Burkett *baseball Hall of Famer*
THE HUMAN CRAB   Johnny "The Trojan" Evers *baseball Hall of Famer*
DESPERATE   Des Beatty *baseball player*
DARK DAYS   James P. Conway *baseball player*
WHAT'S THE USE   Pearce Chiles *baseball player*
BALLOON BUSTER   Frank Luke, Jr. *WWI aviator*
SCREAMIN' JAY   Jalacy Hawkins *singer*
CRYIN'   Sam Collins *bluesman*
WEEPING   Willie Willoughby *baseball player*

1. Gloomy Gus was Tricky Dick's nickname in his college days, when he was wont to escort his girlfriend Pat to dates with other fellows.

THE WEEPING SAINT   Swithin *saint*
THE BEAST OF BELSEN   Irma Grese *Nazi*
THE BITCH OF BUCHENWALD   Ilse Kock *Nazi*
THE MONSTER   Dick Radatz *baseball player*
CAVEMAN   William Lee *fighter*
BRUTE   Victor H. Krulak *Marine general*
BULLY   Preston Smith Brooks *politician*
ROUGH   William Carrigan *baseball catcher, manager*
TOUGH   Tony Anastasio *mobster* / Tony Canzoneri *fighter*
TOUGH GUY   *Texas Gulf Sulfur Co.*
TOUGHIE   Midge Buasuhn *roller derby star*
ROWDY   Joe Lowe *gunfighter*
ROWDY RICHARD   Dick Bartell *baseball player*
SCRAPPY   Russel P. Hartle *U.S. general, WWII*
SAVAGE   Ed Turner *fighter*
WICKED   Wilson Pickett *soul singer*
MEAN   Joe Greene *Pittsburgh Steelers lineman*
NASTY   Ilie Nastase *tennis star*
SID VICIOUS   (John Ritchie) *punk rocker (The Sex Pistols)*
JOHNNY ROTTEN   (John Lydon) *punk rocker (The Sex Pistols)*
THE TERRIBLE TURK   Thomas B. "Czar" Reed *Speaker of the House, aka "Biddy"*
TERRIBLE   Ted Lindsay *hockey player* / Terry McGovern *featherweight champ*
BAD   Henry "Hammerin' Hank" Aaron *home run record holder*
BAD NEWS   Marvin Barnes *basketball player* / James Cato Galloway[2] *baseball player*
BAD BAD LEROY BROWN   Nicky Barnes *underworld figure*
OLD CREEPY   Alvin Karpis *mobster and hitman*
WEIRD   Al Yankovich *novelty singer ("Eat It")*
THE NOB HILL TERROR   Monte Attell *fighter*
SUPERBRAT   John McEnroe *tennis superstar*
CALAMITY JANE   (Martha Jane Burke) *legendary frontier character*
PIFFLES   N. J. Taylor *Canadian football exec*
GENERAL STUBBORNNESS   Vassili Chuikov *Soviet general, WWII*
SNUB   Lawrence Mosley *jazz trombonist*
MIFF   Irving Mole *jazz trombonist*
NERVOUS NORVUS   (Jimmy Drake) *novelty singer ("Transfusion!")*
THE NERVOUS GREEK   Lou Skizas *outfielder*
LONESOME   George Gobel *comedian*
HOMESICK JAMES   James William Henderson *blues singer*

2. Bad News. Galloway was a utility infielder for the 1912 St. Louis Cards. His day job was as a telegraph operator, in which capacity he would send himself wires containing "bad news" so he could leave the office and go play ball.

GABBY   George Francis Hayes *cowboy actor*
BLAB   Bill Schwartz *baseball player*
TALKATIVE TOM   Thomas L. Blanton *Texas politician*
SILENT TOM   Tom Smith *horse trainer*
BASHFUL BROTHER OSWALD   (Beecher "Pete" Kirby) *dobro player*
NAMBY PAMBY   Ambrose Philips *English poet, so dubbed by Pope*
YELLOW   Alcide Nunez *clarinetist*
THE YELLOW KID[3]   Joseph Weil *Chicago con artist*
MUSHY CALLAHAN   (Vincent Morris Scheer) *junior welterweight champ 1926–30*
IFFY THE DOPESTER   Malcolm Bingay *oddsmaker, bookie*
THE MEEK MAN FROM MEEKER   "King" Carl Hubbell, *Hall of Fame pitcher*
WIMPY   (see Cartoon & Other Literary Figures)
CLOWNISH SYCOPHANT   William Wordsworth (see "Blockhead," Head to Toe [Heads])
ME TOO   Thomas C. Platt *politician, aka "Easy Boss"*
BROWN NOSE OF THE YEAR   Jeb Stuart Magruder *Watergate criminal*
MOXIE   Emory Hengle *baseball player*
GUTS   Ishimatsu Suzuki *WBC lightweight champ 1974–76*
COCKY   Alfred Hitchcock *(childhood nickname) aka "The Master of Suspense"*
SPUNKY   Abe Beame *one-time NYC mayor*
FRISKY   Ron William *basketball player*
SASSY   Sarah Vaughan *singer, aka "The Divine Miss Sarah"*
PEP   Ross Youngs *baseball Hall of Famer* / Nathanael West (Nathan Weinstein) *novelist*
WILLIE PEP   Guglielmo *"Will o' the Wisp"* Papelo *featherweight champ 1942–50*
MADCAP MAXIE   Max Baer *heavyweight champ 1934, aka "California Muscleman," "Butcher Boy"*
DEVIL MAY KAER   Morton A. Kaer *football player*
GOOD TIME BILL   William Lamar *outfielder*
PARTY   Stan Partenheimer *pitcher*
WHIMSICAL   Thomas Walker *entertainer*
THE WACKY WARBLER   Joan Turner *comic singer*
HILARIOUS HENRY   Henry Cotton *British golfer*
FUNNY PAPA   John T. Smith *singer*
THE LAUGHING PHILOSOPHER   Democritus *circa 450 B.C.*
LAUGHING   Larry Doyle *NY Giants shortstop 1907–23*
CHUCKLIN'   Charlie O'Rourke *Canadian football player*
SMILIN'   Eddie Hill *Memphis deejay*
SMILIN' ED   Ed McConnell *'50s TV storyteller*

---

3. The Yellow Kid. Joe Weil was so dubbed by Chi-town politician "Bathhouse John" Coughlan. Weil's partner in crime was Fred "The Deacon" Buckminster. Between them they claimed to have flimflammed 2,000 people over forty years. One of Illinois's nicknames is, by the way, "The Sucker State."

SMILING   Mickey Welch *Hall of Fame pitcher*
SMILER   Schuyler Colfax *U. S. Grant's veep*
SMILEY   Lester "Frog" Burnette *cowboy actor* / Lewis (Overton Lemons) *musician*
GRIN   George Bradley *pitcher, 3rd baseman 1876–88*
HAPPY   A. B. Chandler *baseball commissioner* / Margaretta Rockefeller *wife*
HAPPY BOY   Nkosana Mgxaji *South African fighter*
HAPPY JACK   John Hamilton *Dillinger sidekick*
THE HAPPY WARRIOR   Alfred E. Smith *politician, presidential candidate*
THE HAPPY HOOKER   Xaviera Hollander *author*
HAP   Henry Arnold *WWII Army Air Force commander*
JOLLY CHOLLY   Charlie Grimm *aka "The Young Pretender," Cubs 1st baseman 1920–36*
BONNIE PRINCE CHARLIE   Edward Charles Stuart *aka "The Young Pretender," Scottish claimant to the British crown 1720–88*
SWEET   Emma Barrett *blues singer, aka "Sweet Emma the Bell Gal"*
SWEETS   Harry Edison *jazz trumpeter*
SWEETNESS   Walter Payton *Chicago Bears record-holding runningback*
MR. WARMTH   Don Rickles *insult comedian*
THE CHARMER   George Zettlein *pitcher (won 4, lost 20 lifetime)*
GOOD KID   George Susce *baseball player*
COOL PAPA   James Bell *baseball player*
DR. HIP   Eugene Schoenfield *health columnist*
THE HIPSTER   Harry Gibson *musician*
BRAINS   Peter B. Sweeny *crooked politician*
THE BRAIN, THE BIG BRAIN   (see "Mr. Big," Size)
THE BOY GENIUS   Orson Welles *filmmaker*
SLY   Sylvester Stewart Stone *rock star*
SNEAKY   Pete Kleinow *country rock pedal steel guitar player*
PONDEROUS PRIMO   (see "The Ambling Alp," Movement)
DOUBTING   Thomas *apostle*
SILLY BILLY   William IV *English monarch*
DIM DOM   Dom Dallassandro *baseball player*
DAFFY   Paul Dean *pitcher, brother of "Dizzy"*
GOOFY   Vernon "Lefty" Gomez *Hall of Fame pitcher*
DIZZY   Jay Dean *baseball great* / Benjamin Disraeli *British PM* / John Birks Gillespie *jazz great* / Paul Trout *baseball player*
PUTSY   Ralph Caballero *baseball player*
BOOB   Eric McNair *baseball player*
DODO   Michael Marmarosa *musician*
DUM DUM   José Louis Pacheco *fighter*
YO-YO   Pompeyo Davalillo *baseball player*
BOZO   Sterling Bose *trumpeter* / James Shupe *gangster*
BONEHEAD, BLOCKHEAD, DEADHEAD   (see Head to Toe [Heads])

LOCO LOCO   Ricardo Bennett *fighter*
DINGALING   Dain Clay *baseball player*
CUCKOO   Walter "Seacap" Christensen *baseball player*
FOOL TOM   Thomas J. "Stonewall" Jackson *confederate general*
FOOL OF QUALITY   Henry Brooke *novelist*
THE FIGHTING FOOL   (see "Jack Sharkey," Reptiles, Amphibians & Fish)
THE PERFECT FOOL   Ed Wynn *comedian, actor*
CONWAY TWITTY   (Harold Lloyd Jenkins) *country singer*
DIPPY   Don Simmons *hockey player*
SLEEPY   John Estes *bluesman* / Thomas Paulsley LaBeef *country singer*
SLEEPIN'   Sam Hayakawa *California senator*
SNOOZER   Edwin Quinn *guitarist*
JOE BATTY   Joe Batters *criminal*
CRAZY   Joe Gallo *criminal* / Peggy Guggenheim *art patron*
CRAZY ALLEN   Gracie Allen *radio and TV comedienne*
CRAZY OTTO   (Fritz Schulz-Reichel) *pianist*
KILL CRAZY[4]   John Dillinger *bank robber, aka "Public Enemy No. 1"*
PSYCHO   Steve Lyons *baseball player*
MAD   Anthony Wayne *U.S. general*
THE MAD BOMBER   Darryl Lamonica *football player*
THE MADMAN FROM MISSISSIPPI   Gerald Walker *baseball player*
THE MAD MONK   Russ Meyer *baseball player*
THE MAD PROGRAMMER   Marvin Antonowsky *TV exec*
HOWLIN' MAD   Howland Smith *U.S. Marine general, aka "The Pacific Cyclone"*
BOILING BOILY   (see "Ol' Stubble Beard," Head to Toe [Hair])
WILD MAN   Larry Fischer *singer*
WILD BILL   Davison *cornet player* / Donovan *chief of U.S. intelligence, WWII* / (James) Hickok *scout, U.S. marshal, aka "Shanghai Bill," "Duck Bill"*
WOOLY BOB   Robert F. Rich *politician*
OLD FUSS AND FEATHERS   Lieutenant General Winfield Scott *aka "Hero of Chippewa"*
OLD RELIABLE   Tommy Henrich *outfielder*
HONEST ABE, GREATHEART   (see "Honest Abe" Lincoln, U.S. Presidents)
HONEST AVE   Averell "The Crocodile" Harriman *diplomat, politician, son of "The Colossus of Roads"*
HONEST JOHN   John Kelly *baseball umpire*

4. Kill Crazy. John Dillinger was a bank robber by trade, and a remarkably nonviolent one by most accounts. He was implicated in a single murder. But J. Edgar Hoover made him a bogeyman, a terrifying threat to law and order, "Public Enemy No. 1." Dillinger enjoyed a long career of escaping capture and thumbing his nose at G-man No. 1 until he was shot down (unarmed) in the streets. With Kill Crazy's famous penis safely stowed in the Smithsonian, J. Edgar turned his attention to other threats, like Martin Luther King, Jr.

THE TRUTH   Carl Williams *fighter*
OLD TRUE BLUE   Hardy Richardson *baseball player*
GENTLEMAN JIM   James J. Corbett *heavyweight champ 1892–97* / Jim Hickman
   baseball player
GENTLEMANLY   Bobby Clack *baseball player*
SHADY   Bill Leith *baseball player*
PHONEY   Alphonse Martin *right fielder*
THE MAN OF 1,000 FACES   Lon Chaney *actor*

Spring Chickens and Old Coots Department

AGE

THE ELDER   George Coleman, Sr. *English dramatist* / William Pitt, Sr. *English
   statesman*
OLD FOLKS   Herman Pillette *pitcher*
THE OLD MAN   (see "Old Blood and Guts," Assorted Mayhem)
THE NINE OLD MEN   the Disney studio's "heyday"animators / the U.S. Supreme
   Court (pre-"Sandy")
COOT   Orville Veal *shortstop*
BIDDY   Thomas B. "Czar" Reed *Speaker of the House, aka "The Terrible Turk"*
THE ANCIENT   (see "Honest Abe" Lincoln, U.S. Presidents)
THE ANCIENT MARINER   (see Cartoon & Other Literary Figures)
NO KID   Fredrick Glover *hockey player*
THE KID   Jackie Coogan *actor*
BILLY THE KID   William H. Bonney *outlaw, gunslinger, sociopath*
KID ORY   Edward Ory *New Orleans jazz band leader*
KIDDO   George Davis *shortstop 1890–1909, manager*
KID   Hogan Bassey, Jack Berg, Kid Chocolate (Eligio Sardinias), Kid Gavilan (Ger-
   ardo Gonzalez), Perry Graves, Louis Kaplan, George Lavigne, Ted Lewis (Ger-
   shon Mendeloff), Charles McCoy (Norman Selby), Kid Murphy (Peter Frascella),
   Benny Paret, Steve Sullivan, Kid Williams (Johnny Gutenko), Jack Wolfe *cham-
   pion fighters*
THE PITTSBURGH KID   Billy Conn *light heavyweight champ 1939–41*
INFANT[1]   Adrian "Cap" Anson *baseball Hall of Famer*
BABY   Alberto Arizmendi *fighter* / Charles I *king of England*
BABY CORTEZ   (David Clowney) *rock singer*

1. Infant. Adrian Constantine "Cap" Anson was probably the greatest player-manager of
all time. He began his career (with Chicago) in 1876 as "Infant" and wound up twenty-two
seasons and 22,299 put-outs later as "Pop." However, because he refused to play on the same
field as a black man, Negroes were banned from major-league baseball for seventy years.

BABY DOC   Jean-Claude "Baskethead" Duvalier *exiled Haitian dictator*
BABY JAMES   James Taylor *pop singer*
BABY JANE   Jane Holzer, New York disco-socialite
BABY LeROY   (Ronald Overacker) *child actor, nemesis of W. C. Fields*
BABY ZUBIE[2]   Zubin Mehta *orchestra conductor*
BABE   Barbara Paley *socialite* / Vito Parelli *football star* / Eddie Risko *fighter* / Irving Russin *tenor sax player* / Jewell Stovall *singer* / Mildred Didrikson Zaharias *woman athlete of the half-century*
BAMBINO   George Herman "Babe" Ruth, "The Sultan of Swat" *baseball immortal*
THE BLACK BABE RUTH   Josh Gibson *Negro League superstar*
BABE RUTH'S LEGS   (see Head to Toe [Extremities])
TOT[3]   Forest Pressnell *pitcher*
YOUNG CORBETT[4] II   (William H. Rothwell) *featherweight champ 1901*
YOUNG CORBETT III   (Ralph C. Giordano) *welterweight champ 1933*
YOUNG GRIFFO   (Albert Griffiths) *featherweight champ 1890*
YOUNG JACK THOMPSON   (Cecil L. Thompson) *welterweight champ 1930*
THE YOUNGER   George Coleman, Jr. *English dramatist* / William Pitt, Jr. *English statesman*
AGELESS   Johnny Bower *hockey goalie, aka "The China Wall"*

Little Big Men Department

SIZE

BIG   Bill Broonzy *bluesman* / Bill Haywood *wobbly* / Nick Nicholas *musician* / Tom Pendergast *K.C. politico* / Al Sears *sax player* / Maybelle Smith *singer* / Bill Thompson *Chicago mayor 1927–31* / Jim Thompson *Illinois governor* / Bill Tilden *tennis star* / Joe Turner, Joe Williams *singers* / etc.
MR. BIG, THE BIG BANKROLL, THE BIG BRAIN   Arnold Rothstein *criminal, aka "Czar of the Underworld"*
THE BIG BOPPER   (J. P. Richardson) *musician*
BIG KLU, BIG K   Ted Kluzewski *baseball player*
BIG MINH   Duong Van Minh *exiled South Vietnamese general*
BIG WALTER[1]   Walter "Shakey" Horton *bluesman, aka "Mumbles"*

2. Baby Zubie. The sensitive maestro's older brother takes care of the financial end of things.

3. Tot. Pressnell broke in (with the Dodgers) as a thirty-two-year-old rookie. Some tot.

4. Young Corbett. The original Corbett, "Gentleman Jim," took the heavyweight crown from John L. Sullivan in 1892.

1. Big Walter "Shakey" Horton is not to be confused with Little Walter Jacobs, Chicago harmonica master who accompanied Ma Rainey, Howlin' Wolf, Honeybear Edwards, Homesick James, and all the other great nicknames of the era.

BIG SIX[2]   Christy Mathewson *pitching immortal*
BIGGIE   Marshall Goldberg *baseball player*
FAT   Freddie Fitzsimmons   *baseball player* / Jack   Leonard   *comedian* / Tony Salerno *crime boss*
FATS   Joe Berger, Jack Fothergill *baseball players* / Antoine Domino *singer-pianist* / Theodore Navarro *trumpeter* / Thomas Waller *singer-pianist*
FATTY   Roscoe Arbuckle *actor*
FATSO   Bruce Sloan *baseball player*
THE FAT KID   Harmon Killebrew *baseball player*
FATHEAD   David Newman *alto sax player*
TWO TON   Richard Baker *musician* / Tony Galento *criminal*
HEAVY   Paul Blair *baseball player*
HUSKY   Ed Walczak *baseball player*
TUBBY   Alfred Hall *drummer*
CHUBBY CHECKER[3]   (Ernest Evans) *singer*
CHUB   Charles F. Feeney *baseball exec*
PUDGY   (Beverly Cardella) *comedian*
PUDGE[4]   Carlton Fisk *baseball catcher* / James Hefflefinger *football coach*
BLUBBER   Jack Astor *real estate magnate*
JUMBO   Floyd Cummings *fighter*
UNCLE JUMBO, BIG BEEFHEAD, BIG STEVE   (see Cleveland, U.S. Presidents)
THE BROWN BEHEMOTH   (see "The Brown Bomber," Assorted Mayhem)
KINGSIZE   Ted Taylor *musician*
HIS ROTUNDITY   (see John "Old Sink or Swim" Adams, U.S. Presidents)
HUNK   Heartley Anderson *football player, coach*
THE BLIMP   Ernest G. Phelps *politician*
THE ROUND MAN   Ron Northey *baseball player*
MR. 5 × 5   Jimmy Rushing *singer*
HORSE BELLY   Joe Sargent *baseball player*
MAN MOUNTAIN DEAN   (Frank S. Levitt) *wrestler*
THE TOWERING CLIFF OF BLACK MOUNTAIN   Cliff "Mountain Music" Melton *baseball player*
THE TALL TACTICIAN   Connie Mack (Cornelius McGillicuddy) *baseball owner, manager*
TOO-TALL   Ed Jones *fighter, football player*

2. Big Six. A reference to a celebrated speedy firetruck of the time, hence a compliment to Christy's fastball.
3. Chubby. Mr. Evans shamelessly fashioned his pseudonym on the nickname and real name of Fats Domino, leading rock fans at the time to anticipate "Pudgy Parcheesi" and "Man Mountain Monopoly" . . .
4. Pudge Hefflefinger devised a defensive strategy against the "Flying Wedge." He jumped onto the man leading it.

LONG JOHN   John Baldry *British rock star* / John Neeble *New York radio personality*

LONG TOM   (see Jefferson, U.S. Presidents)

THE LONG 'UN, THE TALL SUCKER   (see "Honest Abe" Lincoln, U.S. Presidents)

INCH   Frank Gleich *baseball player*

STRETCH   Willie Lee McCovey *baseball Hall of Famer*

10½ INCHES   Mark Stevens *porn actor*

THE POTAWATOMI GIANT   (see "Great White Hope," Superlatives)

ANDRE THE GIANT   (Andre Roussimoff) *wrestler*

LITTLE GIANT   Stephen Douglas *politician, orator*

BIG TINY LITTLE   Dudley Little *musician*

TINY   Nate "The Skate" Archibald *basketball player* / Lloyd Grimes *guitarist*

WEE   Bea Booze *singer* / Willie ("Hit 'Em Where They Ain't") Keeler *baseball player*

PEE WEE   Ernie Dunbar, Robert Rucker, Arcadio Suarez *fighters* / Walter Hunt, Charles Russel *jazz musicians* / Harold "The Little Colonel" Reese[5] *baseball player*

PEEWEE HERMAN   (Paul Reubens) *comedian, actor*

SKINNY   Jonathan M. Wainwright *WWII general*

SLIM   Otis Dewey Whitman *yodeler*

SLIM HARPO   (James Moore) *musician, singer*

SLIM PICKENS   (Louis B. Lindley, Jr.) *actor*

GUITAR SLIM   (Eddie Jones) *musician*

SUNNYLAND SLIM   (Albert Luandrew) *singer, aka "Delta Joe"*

YODELIN' SLIM   Raymond LeRoy Clarke *C&W singer*

SHORTY   Harold Baker, Milton M. Rogers *musicians* / Hugh Ray *NFL official*

MIDGET WOLGAST   (Joseph Loscalzo) *fighter*

DINK   Ollie Johnson *pianist* / George Lewis "Tex" Rickard[6] *sports promoter, aka "Master of Ballyhoo"* / Robert L. Templeton *football and track coach*

RUNT   Cecil W. Bishop *Illinois politician*

HALF PINT   Frankie Jaxon *singer* / Gene Rye *baseball player*

BITSY, THE ATLANTA ATOM   Bryan Grant *tennis player*

LOW   Lloyd Christenbury *baseball player*

HAIRBREADTH HARRY   Jack Hamilton *baseball player*

LITTLE   Anthony (Anthony Gourdine) *singer* / Chis (Elijah Chism) *baseball player* / Eva (Eva Boyd) *singer* / Milton (Milton Campbell) *singer* / Mo (Maureen Connolly) *tennis champ* / Richard (Richard Penniman) *rock & roll pioneer* /

---

5. Brooklyn Dodger Pee Wee Reese was named not for his size (he was 5'10" and towered over his crosstown rival shortstop Phil "Scooter" Rizzuto). He picked up the nickname as a boy marbles champion.

6. Dink. Because "Tex" Rickard operated Madison Square Garden, the New York hockey team was named, incongruously, Rangers. Tex's Rangers. Get it?

Steven (Steve Van Zandt) *musician, formerly "Miami Steve Van Zandt"* / Stevie (Stevie Wonder, born Steveland Morris) *musician, singer* / Walter (Walter Jacobs) *bluesman* / Willie John (Willie John Woods) *singer*

LITTLE   Albie Booth *football, aka "Little Boy Blue," "The Mighty Mite"* / Jimmy Dickens *country singer* / Jimmy Scott *Opry singer* / Billy Smith *Broadway vaudevillian*

They Often Call Me Speedo Department

MOVEMENT

TRAVELIN'   Travis Tidwell *Giants QB*

THE ARKANSAS TRAVELER   Bob Burns *vaudeville comic*

WALKIN'   Dan Walker *Illinois governor*

THE WALKING MAN   Eddy Yost *baseball player*

WANDERING   Eric Brook *British soccer player*

RAMBLIN'   Willard Thomas *bluesman*

RAMBLIN' JACK ELLIOTT   (Elliot Adnopoz) *country musician*

SCRAMBLIN'   Fran Tarkenton *football QB, aka "Sir Francis"*

SHUFFLIN'   Phil Douglas *baseball player*

LEAPIN'[1]   Lena Levinsky *fight manager and handler*

JUMPING   Joe Williams, Joe Savoldi *football players*

JUMPING JACK   Daniel Jones *baseball player*

SLIDING   Billy Hamilton *baseball player*

BOUNDING   Betty Nuthall *tennis player*

THE BOUNDING BASQUE   Jean Borotra *tennis player*

THE GALLOPING GHOST   Harold "Red" Grange *football immortal*

THE GALLOPING GOURMET   Graham Kerr *television chef*

THE AMBLING ALP   Primo Carnera *heavyweight champ 1933–34, aka "The Vast Venetian," "Ponderous Primo"*

HOPALONG   Howard Cassady *football player*

HIPPETTY HOPP   John Hopp *baseball player*

STEPIN FETCHIT   (Lincoln Perry) *actor*

THE STEPPER   Fred Harris *fighter*

THE CREEPER   Ed Stroud *baseball player*

THE CRUISER, THE GLIDER, SCOOTER   (see Getting There)

COASTER JOE   Joseph Connolly *baseball player*

1. Leapin' Lena. She handled the promotional side of her brother's unusual prize-fighting career. He was Battling "King" Levinsky, born Barney Lebrowitz, light heavyweight champion from 1916 to 1920. King had 274 fights—176 of them were to no decision. Often they were exhibition bouts, as the brother-sister pair barnstormed across the country, Levinsky fighting all comers—sometimes three a day—and Lena in his corner, leaping.

WHIZZER   Byron White *Supreme Court justice*

THE FOWLERVILLE FLAILER   Charles "The Mechanical Man" Gehringer *baseball Hall of Famer*

CARTWHEEL   Wilburn Cartwright *politician*

ROGER THE DODGER, CLYDE THE GLIDE, SHUNT HUNT   (see Rhymers)

SLIDE   Locksley Hampton *trombonist*

SKIP   Nehemiah James *bluesman*

FLIP   Phillips (Joseph E. Filipelli) *jazz musician* / Al Rosen *baseball player* / Clerow Wilson *comedian, actor*

SLIP   Edward P. Maddigan *football coach*

RISE UP   William Allen (see "The Ohio Gong," Native Sons)

MOVE UP JOE   John "Joe" Gerhardt *baseball player*

POOSH 'EM UP   Tony Lazzeri *baseball player*

STEADYROLL   James P. Johnson *pianist*

SLOW DRAG   Alcide Pavageau *bassist*

TWITCH   Marv Rickert *baseball player*

OLD SHAKE   William Shakespeare *dramatist, poet, aka "The Bard of Avon"*

SHAKEY   (see "Big Walter," Size)

SHOOK   Elmer Brown *pitcher*

FIDGETY   Phil Collins *pitcher*

JITTERY   Joe Berry *pitcher*

HERKY JERKY   Elmer Horton *baseball player*

ZIGGY   Harry Elman *trumpeter*

FLIP FLAP   Oscar Jones *baseball player*

STEADY EDDIE LOPAT, STILL BILL HILL (see Rhymers)

GO   Hisami Numata *fighter*

QUICK   James Tillis *fighter*

RAPID ROBERT   Bob Feller *pitcher, aka "Bullet Bob"*

SPEED   Magee (Harold Johnson) *editor* / Lawrence Webb *drummer*

SPEEDO   Earl Carroll *rock musician*

SPEEDY   Achille Mitchell *fighter*

SWIFTY   Irving Lazar *agent*

ZOOMIE   Elmo Zumwalt *U.S. admiral*

DASH   Dashiell Hammett *writer*

ZIP   Prisciliano Castillo *fighter* / George Zabel *pitcher*

FLASH   Gabriel Elorde *fighter* / Joe Gordon *baseball player*

THE FORDHAM FLASH   Frank Frisch *baseball player*

THE PURPLE STREAK   Ben Boynton *football player*

CHARLIE HUSTLE   Pete Rose *baseball player, manager*

TROTS   Bryan Trottier *hockey player*

SKIDS   Johnny Lipon *baseball player*

HURRYIN'   Hugh McElhenny *football player*

HURRY UP   Fielding H. Yost *football coach, aka "Point-a-Minute"*

HURRY UP HENRY   Henry J. Kaiser *auto magnate*
MICK THE QUICK, SLOE JOE   (see Rhymers)
BACKWARDS   Sam Firke *blues guitarist*
WRONGWAY REIGELS   W. W. Reigels *football player, ran the wrong way at the Rose Bowl, '20s. Not to be confused with "Wrongway Corrigan," the pilot who flew from NY to Ireland in 1938. He was headed for LA.*
BYE BYE   Steve Balboni *baseball slugger*

Good 'n' Plenty Department

SUPERLATIVES

ACE OF ACES   Eddie Rickenbacker *American flying ace*
ACE OF SPIES   Sidney Reilly *spy*
THE ADMIRABLE   James Crichton *British savant*
ADMIRABLE DOCTOR   Roger Bacon *philosopher*
AMAZING   Willie Mays *baseball player, aka "The Say Hey Kid"*
THE AMAZING KRESKIN   (George Kresge) *mentalist*
THE AMAZING RANDI   (James Randi) *debunker of "mentalists," MacArthur Foundation "Genius Grant" recipient, 1986*
AMERICA'S FAVORITE COWBOY   Tom Mix *actor*
AMERICA'S MOST PERFECTLY DEVELOPED MAN   Charles Atlas (Angelo Siciliano) *bodybuilder, businessman*
AMERICA'S NO. 1 HOSTESS   Elsa Maxwell *bon vivant*
AMERICA'S PREMIER AIR WOMAN   Amelia Earhart (Putnam) *aviatrix*
ART THE GREAT, WHATAMAN   Charles Arthur Shires *baseball player*
BEAUTIFUL   Bob Taylor *actor*
BEAUTY[1]   Dave Bancroft *baseball player*
BLACK BEAUTY   (see "The Brown Bomber," Assorted Mayhem)
CAPABILITY   Lancelot Brown *18th-century British gardener*
CHAMP   James Clark *Speaker of the House*
CHAMPION   Jack Dupree *singer, musician*
CLIMAX   Clarence Blethen *baseball player*
DANDY   Don Meredith *quarterback, sports announcer*
DASHING DONS   Don Geyer and Don Heap *football players*
THE DAPPER DON   John Gotti *reputed mob leader, aka "The Good Looking Guy"*
DIVINE   (Glen Milstead) *actor, actress*
THE DIVINE   Sarah Bernhardt *actress, aka "Madame Damala"*
THE DIVINE MISS   Sarah "Sassy" Vaughan *singer*

---

1. Beauty. Hall of Fame 3rd baseman Bancroft was not, in fact, pulchritudinous, but would shout "Beauty" whenever a nice play was made.

THE DIVINE MS. M   Bette Midler *singer, actress*
DEAN THE DREAM   Dean Meminger *basketball player*
DYNAMO   Dino Chiozza *hitless baseball player*
DAVE THE EDGE   Dave Evans *rock musician*
ELEGANT   Abraham Oakey Hall *crooked New York mayor*
THE FAB FOUR   The Beatles *aka "The Mop Tops"*
FIRST LADY OF THE THEATER   Helen Hayes (Helen Brown) *actress*
FOOL OF QUALITY   Henry Brooke *novelist*
THE FRESHEST MAN ON EARTH   Walter "Arlie" Latham *3rd baseman*
GOD   (see "Father Divine," Religion & Mystery)
GORGEOUS GEORGE (George R. Wagner) *wrestler*
GORGEOUS GEORGE, THE PERFECT BALLPLAYER   George Sisler *baseball
    player, aka "The Brown Blaster"*
THE GORGEOUS GREETER   Grover "Gardenia" Whalen *politician, businessman*
THE GREAT BEAST   Edward "Alistair" Crowley *diabolist*
THE GREAT COMMONER   William Pitt (the Elder) *British statesman*
THE GREAT COMPROMISER   Henry "Same Old Coon" Clay *statesman*
THE GREAT EMANCIPATOR   (see "Honest Abe" Lincoln, U.S. Presidents) / Daniel
    O'Connell *Irish politician*
THE GREAT GARBO   Greta Garbo (Greta Gustafsson) *movie actress*
THE GREAT GABBO   (see "Little Beau Peep," Cartoon & Other Literary Figures)
THE GREAT GLORIFIER   Flo Ziegfeld *showman*
THE GREAT GROANER   (see "The Croon Prince," Assumed Titles)
THE GREAT HAMMERER   (see "Butcher" Ulysses S. Grant, U.S. Presidents)
GREATHEART   (see "Honest Abe" Lincoln, U.S. Presidents)
THE GREAT IMPOSTOR   William Weinberg *criminal impersonator*
THE GREAT LOVER   Valentino (see Love & Sex)
THE GREAT NULLIFIER   John Calhoun *champion of states' rights*
THE GREAT ONE   Jackie Gleason *actor, comedian*
THE GREAT ORATOR   William Jennings "Boy" Bryan *aka "The Great Commoner,"
    "Silver Tongue"*
THE GREAT PROFILE   John Barrymore (John Blythe) *actor*
THE GREAT THUNDERING ROOSTER   U. S. "Crackdown" Johnson *FDR cabinet
    member*
THE GREAT WHITE CHIEF   (see "Bullmoose" Teddy Roosevelt, U.S. Presidents)
THE GREAT WHITE HOPE   Jess Willard *heavyweight champ 1915–19, aka "The
    Potawatomi Giant"*
THE GREAT   John "Duster" Mails *pitcher*
THE GREATEST   Muhammad Ali (see "The Louisville Lip," Head to Toe [Mouths])
HANDSOME   Dick Manitoba *pop singer*
THE HEAVENLY TWINS   Hugh Duffy and Tommy McCarthy *baseball players*
HER NIBS MISS GEORGIA GIBBS   *singer*
THE IDOL OF BASEBALL FANDOM   Ty Cobb *aka "The Georgia Peach"*

IDOL OF OHIO   (see McKinley, U.S. Presidents)
THE IMMORTAL   Jose Azcue *baseball player*
THE INVINCIBLE ONE   Warren Spahn *pitcher*
THE IT GIRL   (see Girls)
LITTLE ALL RIGHT   Claude Cassius Ritchey *baseball player*
LITTLE SURE SHOT   Annie Oakley *sharpshooter*
LUSCIOUS   Lucius Beebe *columnist, bon vivant*
MARVELOUS   Marvin Hagler *fighter*
THE MASTER OF SUSPENSE   Alfred Hitchcock *director*
MR. WONDERFUL   Sammy Davis, Jr. *entertainer*
NAILS   Len Dykstra *baseball ("Nails" is Dykstraese for "awesome")*
THE NONPAREIL   Jack Dempsey (John Kelly) *middleweight champ 1884–91*
THE ONLY   Edward Nolan *baseball player*
THE PEERLESS LEADER   Frank Chance *Hall of Fame baseball manager*
THE PEOPLE'S CHERCE[2]   "Dixie" Fred Walker *baseball player*
THE PERFECT FOOL   Ed Wynn *comedian, actor*
PHENOMENAL   John Smith *pitcher*
PRETTY   Bernard Purdie *drummer*
PRETTY BOY   Charles Arthur Floyd *gangster*
PRETTY PERKY   Peggy King *singer*
PRIDE OF THE GHETTO   Joe Bernstein *fighter*
DAVE THE RAVE   Dave Stallworth *basketball player*
RAZZLE DAZZLE   Con Murphy *pitcher*
THE SPLENDID SPLINTER   (see Wood)
SUPERBRAT   John McEnroe *tennis superstar*
SUPERCHIEF   Allie Reynolds *baseball player*
SUPERFOOT   Bill Wallace *high-kick karate champ*
SUPERJEW   Mike Epstein *baseball player*
SUPERKRAUT   Henry "Henry the K" Kissinger *diplomat*
SUPERMEX   Lee Trevino *golfer*
THE $10,000 BEAUTY   Mike "King" Kelly *baseball player*
TOM TERRIFIC   Tom Seaver *pitcher*
PHIL THE THRILL   Phil Sellers *basketball player*
WONDERFUL   Floyd Smith *jazz musician* / Willie Smith *baseball player*

THE PITS

USELESS   (see "Butcher" Ulysses S. Grant, U.S. Presidents)
UNKNOWN   Edward Winston *'30s heavyweight*

---

2. The People's Cherce. Dixie refused to play on the same team as Jackie Robinson, and it was Walter O'Malley's cherce to send the popular outfielder to the Pirates.

UGLY   Baruk Levy *fighter*
BAD BODY   Thurman Munson *baseball player, aka "Squatty"*
LOSING PITCHER   Hugh "Duke" Mulcahy *baseball great*
WHOOPS   Pat Creeden *baseball player*
OH! OH!   Orlando Woolridge *basketball player*
CLINKERS   Bill Fagan *pitcher*
THE TRUMPED-UP   Philip (VI) Valois *French King, reigned 1328–50*
BROWN NOSE OF THE YEAR   (see Attitudes)
THE SCHMALTZ KING   Guy "Mr. New Year's Eve" Lombardo *bandleader*
THE MAN YOU LOVE TO HATE   Erich Von Stroheim *director*
THE LESSER   James *apostle*

The Great, the Bad and the Ugly Department

HISTORICAL "GREATS"

Many of the 861 Greats earned the envied title by begetting heirs in times of scarcity, several earned it by generalship in war and other forms of massacre, others earned it by illustrious achievements in the line of Benevolent Assimilation, still others by acting as the Church's harlot, others still by enriching the nobility with State lands and with large pensions and gratuities bilked from the public till; the rest earned it by sitting still, looking wise, accepting the credit for the great achievements of their ministers of State—and not meddling.

—Mark Twain, aka Samuel Clemens,
Three Thousand Years Among the Microbes

History, or historians, or public relations firms, whatever, have indeed awarded the sobriquet "The Great" to many rulers and saints in mankind's illustrious past. The following celebrities are usually listed as such in that encyclopedia over there, the one you've been using as a doorstop . . .

AKBAR THE GREAT (1542–1605). Third of the Mongol emperors, Akbar conquered all of India, not to mention Afghanistan, with maximum carnage. Great, moreover, was his love of learning. In the course of his pillaging, he collected a library of 24,000 volumes. And doubtless he would have read them, if he'd ever learned how.

ALEXANDER THE GREAT (356–323 B.C.). Slaughtered the odd close relative (including his father Philip), most of his close friends, and innumerable total strangers, including many thousands of Indians (he began the tradition). When drunk, Alex was inclined to incinerate cities. He allegedly wept with chagrin when he'd run out of foreigners to subjugate. Known in his time as "The Madman of Macedonia."

ALFRED THE GREAT (849–99). After the invading Saxons killed, enslaved, or threw out the native Picts of England, the Saxon King Alfred fought to keep the Danes away, under the slogan "England for the English." Al is beloved in jolly old song and legend for having let the oat cakes burn, thereby inventing British cooking.

ANTIOCHUS THE GREAT (242–187 B.C.). Chief of a minor-league tribe in Asia minor, did a six-year rape-and-pillage act in homage to his hero Alexander (see above). Antiochus was called "The Great" by Roman generals, the better to glorify their easy military victories over him.

BASIL THE GREAT (330–79). The founder of Western monasticism, he made up rules so that hermits wishing only to be left alone could live together in large groups.

CATHERINE THE GREAT (1729–96). Czarina of All the Russias, she was known as "Little Mother," neither of which was true. German by birth, she spoke French. A woman of considerable libido, she had her First Minister Potemkin select her prospective one-night-stands from among the palace guard. Candidates were then screened by a physician and test-driven by her ladies-in-waiting. (Catherine did not, contrary to the popular myth, expire in the embraces of a stallion.)

CHARLES THE GREAT (Charlemagne) (742–814). Founder of the Holy Roman Empire—which was unholy, French, and at best a loose and temporary alliance of warlords. Charlemagne married nine times, but there was no one quite like his mom, "Big Foot Bertha." They say he was eight feet tall and could bend horseshoes with his bare hands. They also say he could read a little bit.

CONSTANTINE THE GREAT (280–337). First Roman emperor to be converted to Christianity, he was thus the first to call for all-out slaughter in the name of the Cross, setting an example for presidents, generals, and coaches to this day. His shameless politicizing and secularization of the Gospel accounted for the activities of Basil the Great (see above).

FREDERICK THE GREAT (1712–86). King of Prussia, military monster, and culture vulture. Freddy invaded all his neighbors except France, to which he sucked up.

GREGORY THE GREAT (540–604). Pope from 590 to 604. Tried hard to reform the monasteries of Basil (see above) and the empire of Constantine (see above). Created the form of moaning heard, until recently, in Roman Catholic churches—Gregorian chant—but he had nothing whatever to do with the Gregorian calendar.

HEROD THE GREAT (73–4 B.C.). Jewish king who collaborated with the Roman occupation forces. Murdered his wife, children, John the Baptist, and all the male infants in Judea. Nice.

IVAN THE GREAT (1440–1505). The third grand duke of Muscovy, grand-father of Ivan the Terrible, this Vasilyevich banished from the Motherland the last Mongol invaders (see Akbar the Great, above). Ivan's failed economic and expansionist policies nevertheless resulted in serfdom in Russia, dragged her forward into feudalism and, with Hegelian inevitability, toward the creation of the Workers' Paradise.

LEO THE GREAT (400–61). Pope from 440 to 461. Venerated for his powers of diplomacy. Leo asked Attila the Hun to please go away from the gates of Rome . . . and whataya know, the old "Scourge of God" did just that!

PETER THE GREAT (1672–1725). Czar of Russia, he was determined to civilize the place. Had his own son and his brother-in-law murdered; decapitated anyone growing a beard; set a fine example for backward serfs.

POMPEY THE GREAT (106–48 B.C.). A great statesman of the Roman Empire. Pompey became filthy rich as chief enforcer for the international protection racket the Imperial Senate and Army were then running in Asia Minor and on the High Seas. Pompey got away with double-crossing Sulla, Crassus, and Lepidus, then tried his old partner Julius Caesar, got bumped off soon, quietly and out of town. Same old story (see *The Godfather*).

THEODOSIUS THE GREAT (347–95). Emperor at Byzantium, he briefly reunited the Roman Empire by capturing and executing his Western rival, the humbly titled Magnus Maximus. Theodosius was a good Christian. He ordered the slaughter of 7,000 Thesalonian men, women, and children, but later said he was sorry. He is often confused with *THEODORIC THE GREAT (450–526),* king of the Ostrogoths, a barbarian who finally stomped Rome into the ground, undoing the work of many of the above "Greats," but setting history's stage for others.

8

THE CAPTAINS AND THE KINGS

The higher civilization a nation possesses, the less a need for nicknames is felt, and the ones coined are more on the polite side. In the U.S. today, nicknames are heard chiefly among participants in team sports, in the school yard, and among the criminal element.
— Elsdon C. Smith (president of the American Names Society)
American Surnames (1979)

Tippecanoe and the Gipper, Too Department

U.S. PRESIDENTS

George "Old Fox" Washington, aka "The Farmer President," "The Surveyor President," "Stepfather of His Country"

John "Old Sink or Swim" Adams, aka "His Rotundity," "His Superfluous Excellency"

"Long Tom" Jefferson, aka "The Red Fox," "The Sage of Monticello"

"Jemmy" Madison, aka "Great Little Jim," "The Berserker"

James "Mere Imagination" Monroe, aka "The Last Cocked Hat"

"King John the Second" Quincy Adams, aka "Old Man Eloquent," "The Massachusetts Madman"

"Old Hickory" Andy Jackson, aka "King Andrew the First," "Duel Fighter," "The Sage of the Hermitage," "The Pointed Arrow," "The Sharp Knife"

"Little Van" Matty "Old Kinderhook" Van Buren, aka "The Little Magician," "The Petticoat Pet," "The Kinderhook Fox," "Whiskey Van," "Mistletoe Politician," "The Weasel"

William "Tippecanoe" Harrison, aka "Hard Cider," "Old Granny," "General Mum," "Log Cabin Candidate"

"Old Veto" John Tyler, aka "His Accidency," "The Executive Ass"

"Dark Horse" Jim Polk, aka "The Plodder," "The Napoleon of the Stump"

"Old Rough and Ready" Zack Taylor, aka "Old Buena Vista"

Millard "The Wool-Carder" Fillmore, aka "The Handsome Mediocrity," "The Accidental President"

"The Fainting General" Franklin Pierce, aka "Purse," "Hero of Many a Hard-Fought Bottle"

"Ten Cent" Jimmy Buchanan, aka "Old Buck," "The Old Functionary," "The Bachelor President," "Sage of Wheatland"

"Honest Abe" Lincoln, aka "The Rail Splitter," "The Original Gorilla," "The Great Emancipator," "Massa Linkum," "The Tall Sucker," "The Long 'Un," "The Illinois Ape," "Baboon," "Tycoon," "The Ancient"

"The Drunken Tailor" Andy Johnson, aka "Sir Veto," "Lord of Misrule," "Daddy of the Baby," "Father of the Homestead"

"Butcher" Ulysses S. Grant, aka "Hug," "Useless," "United States," "Unconditional Surrender," "The Tanner President," "Uncle Sam," "The Great Hammerer," "The Silent Man"

"His Fraudulency" Rutherford B. "Granny" Hayes, aka "Dark Horse," "The Usurper," "Old 8 to 7"

"Canal Boy" James Garfield, aka "The Preacher," "The Available Man," "The Teacher President"

Chet "The Dude" Arthur, aka "Prince Arthur," "A Nonentity with Side-Whiskers"

Grover "The Buffalo Hangman" (or "Sheriff") Cleveland, aka "Uncle Jumbo," "Big Beefhead," "Big Steve," "Stuffed Prophet," "Dumb Prophet," "The Perpetual Candidate," "The Claimant," "The Buxom Buffalonian," "His Obstinacy"

"Chinese" Ben Harrison, aka "Grandfather's Hat," "Iceberg," "Kid Gloves," "Another Falstaff," "Baby McKee's Grandfather"

William "The Stockingfoot Orator" McKinley, aka "The Idol of Ohio," "Prosperity's Advance Agent," "A Chocolate Eclair," "Wobbly Willie"

"Bullmoose" Teddy Roosevelt, aka "That Damned Cowboy," "Telescope Teddy," "Four Eyes," "Theodore the Meddler," "Trust-Buster," "Rough Rider," "The Great White Chief," "Wielder of the Big Stick"

William Howard "God Knows" Taft, aka "Big Chief"

Woody "Doc" Wilson, aka "The Professor," "Coiner of Weasel Words"

Warren "Winnie" Harding, aka "The He-Harlot," "Bungalow-Mind"

"Silent" Cal Coolidge, aka "Red"

Bert Hoover, aka "Friend of the Helpless Children"

Franklin "Boss" Roosevelt, aka "That Man in the White House," "Mr. Big," "Sphinx," "The Roosecrat," "The Alphabet Soup-Kitcheneer," "FDR," "Kangaroosevelt"

"Give 'em Hell" Harry Truman, aka "Haberdasher Harry"

Dwight D. "Ike" Eisenhower, aka "Ugly Ike," "The Great Golfer"

Jack Kennedy, aka "Washington's Gay Young Bachelor," "JFK"

"Landslide" Lyndon Johnson, aka "LBJ The Nice," "LBJ The Tough," "Big Daddy,"
    "Lightbulb Lyndon," "Uncle Cornpone"
"Tricky" Dick Nixon, aka "Gloomy Gus"
Jimmy "Hots" Carter, aka "The Peanut Farmer," "Grits"
Gerry "Junie" Ford (born Leslie Lynch King, Jr.), aka "Dum-Dum," "Mister Clean"
Ron "Dutch" Reagan, aka "The Great Communicator," "The Teflon President," "The
    Gipper"

THE FIRST LADIES

Martha Washington answered to "Lady."
Dorothea Madison was better known as "Dolley."
Jane Pierce never appeared in public, was "The Shadow in the White House."
Mary Todd Lincoln was known as "The She-Wolf."
Lucy Hayes would not serve liquor, earning herself the title "Lemonade Lucy."
Helen Taft was "Nellie."
Edith Wilson was "The First Lady President," it was said.

Warren and the nation referred to Florence Harding as "The Duchess."

Republicans discovered Mrs. Truman was on salary, dubbed her "Payroll Bess."

Claudia Johnson (née Taylor) grew up with the nickname "Lady Bird," it being alleged that when young she was "purty" as one.

Thelma Nixon was "Pat"; twice her husband appeared on TV to deplore the custom of calling her "Plastic Pat," which no one (except maybe Dick, Bebe, and the boys) actually ever did.

Rosalynn Carter was, inevitably, "The Steel Magnolia."

Ann Frances Reagan is "Nancy" to the world, but "Mommy" to her "Daddy."

THE VEEPS

Teddy Roosevelt's second-in-command was the undemonstrative Charles "Icebanks" Fairbanks; Taft's was the affable "Sunny Jim" Sherman.

Doc Wilson's vice president was Thomas "Five-Cent Cigar" Marshall (who first observed, "What this country needs . . ."). Hoover was seconded by Charles "Big Chief" Curtis, supposedly of American Indian descent.

For his first term, FDR chose John Nance Garner as his vice president. In the Golden Age of Nicknames, the '30s, Garner was "Cactus Jack," "Mohair Jack," "The Owl," and "Poker Face." Roosevelt's second term VP was Henry "Plow 'em Under" Wallace, former Secretary of Agriculture.

Alben Barkley, who served under Truman, was the first to be called "Veep."

LBJ's man was Hubert H. Humphrey, "Pinky" to his pals, "The Happy Warrior" to his constituents, and "The Hump" to those who wanted him dumped.

Abbie Hoffman insisted on calling Nixon's Agnew "Spiro T. Eggplant."

Jimmy Carter's vice president was Walter "Fritz" Mondale, who, with vice-presidential candidate Geraldine Ferraro, formed half the team of "Fritz 'n' Tits," or "Wally and the Beaver."

Monarchical Monikers Department

THE CROWNED HEADS OF EUROPE

One night it happened that he took
A peep at an old history book,
Wherein he came across, by chance,
A picture of a King of France.
(A stoutish man), and, down below
These words, "King Louis So-and-So,
Nicknamed 'The Handsome' "! There he sat,
And (think of it!) the man was fat!

—A. A. Milne,
When We Were Very Young

The Royals

"Harefoot" Harold, "Dollheart" John, "Longshanks" Edward, "Crouchback" Richard, "Old Ironsides" Cromwell, "Dutch Billy," "Dapper George" and "Old Rowley." Would you believe a baseball team made up of these guys? No? How about a cricket side? Would you believe the kings of England? Okay.

Here are a thousand years of royal British nicknames:

Alfred "The Great," aka "England's Darling"
Edward "The Elder," aka "The Magnificent"
Athelstan "The Glorious"
Edmund I
Eadred[1]
Eadwig "The Fair"
Edgar "The Peaceable"
Edward "The Martyr"
Ethelred "The Unready"[2]
Edmund II "Ironside"
Canute "The Dane," aka "The Great"
Harold I "Harefoot"
Canute II "Hardecanute," aka "Hathacanute"
Edward "The Confessor"
Harold II "The Last of the Saxons"

---

1. Eadred (946–55) had no nickname. His competition for the throne, Eric "Bloodaxe," had a beauty, though.
2. Ethelred (979–1016) got his famous "Unready" tag through a mistranslation. "Unraed" means "ill-advised," "illiterate," or "thick as a brick."

William I "The Conqueror," aka "The Bastard"
William II "Rufus" ("Redhead")
Henry I "Beauclerc" ("Good Student")
Stephen[3]
Henry II "Plantagenet" ("Broom Plant"), aka "Curtmantle" ("Short Cape")
Richard I "Lionheart,"[4] aka "Old Yea and Nay"
John "Lackland," aka "Softsword," "Dollheart"
Henry III "The Old King"
Edward "Longshanks," aka "The Hammer of the Scots," "The English Justinian"
Edward II[5]
Edward III "The Bankrupt"
Richard II[6]
Henry IV[7]
Henry V "Harry," aka "The English Alexander"
Henry VI "The Ill-Fated," aka "The Martyr"
Edward IV "The Robber"
Edward V "The Prince in the Tower"
Richard III "Crouchback," aka "The Hog," "The Boar," "Crookback"
Henry VII "Panurgus"
Henry VIII "Bluff King Hal," aka "Bo-Ho," "Stout Harry"
Edward VI "The Saint"
Jane Grey "Queen of Nine Days"
"Bloody" Mary
Elizabeth I "Good Queen Bess," aka "The Virgin Queen," "Glorianna," "The Untamed Heifer"[8]
James I "The Wisest Fool in Europe"

3. King Stephen (1135–54) had a dubious claim to the throne, which probably belonged to Matilda, known as "Empress Maude." Stephen's reign got a nickname: "The Anarchy."

4. Richard "Lionheart" was held in less esteem by his troops than by modern day fans of Robin Hood (Robert of Locksley, aka Robin Wood) movies. His officers called him "Yea and Nay"—he wasn't the decisive sort.

5. History does not record the many nicknames Edward II's flamboyant homosexuality doubtless earned him before 1327, when he was deposed. His unhappy wife was Isabella "The She-Wolf of France."

6. Richard II, grandson of Edward III and son of "The Black Prince," assumed the throne, aged thirty-four, in 1377. He had to deal with the bubonic plague, and rebellions by John "The Mad Priest" Ball and Walter "Wat" Tyler, and just wasn't up to it. Deposed, 1399.

7. Henry IV, son of John "of Gaunt," usurped the throne, and thereafter defeated the Welsh rebel Henry "Hotspur" Percy.

8. In 1593, one John Perry was beheaded for having called Queen Elizabeth I "The Untamed Heifer," a reference to her spinsterhood. Somewhat later, Edmund Spenser was knighted for dubbing her "Glorianna, The Faerie Queene." The Age of Public Relations was born.

Charles I "Baby,"[9] aka "The Last Man," "The White King"
Oliver Cromwell "Old Ironsides"
Richard Cromwell "Queen Dick"
Charles II "Old Rowley," aka "The Merry Monarch," "Blackbird"
James II[10] "The Popish Duke"
William III "Dutch Billy"
Anne "Brandy Nan"
George I "The Turnip Hoer"
George II "The Dapper"
George III "Old Nobs," aka "German Georgie," "Farmer George"
George IV[11] "Florizel," aka "Prinney," "The Fat Adonis," "Prince of Whales"
William IV "Silly Billy," aka "Sailor Bill"
Victoria[12] "The Widow at Windsor"

9. Charles I's nickname "Baby" found its way into the nursery rhyme, "Rockabye Baby." When he was beheaded, down, indeed, came Baby, cradle and all.

10. In 1688 James II became "The King over the Water," or "Old Pretender." Among his descendants was Charles "Bonnie Prince Charlie."

11. The poet George "Mad, Bad and Dangerous to Know" Gordon (Lord Byron) dubbed George the Fourth "Fum."

12. Queen Victoria, upon the demise of her husband "Dear Albert," aka "Albert the Good," went into lifelong mourning. The otherwise patriotic poet Rudyard Kipling dubbed her "The Widow at Windsor," and thus was denied the poet laureatship, or so the story goes.

Edward VII "Bertie the Rake," aka "Uncle of Europe"
George V "The Well-Beloved"
Edward VIII "David," aka "The Abdicator," "Teddie," "A Boy"
George VI "Bertie"
Elizabeth II "The Sov," aka "Brenda," "HM"

Noms d'un Nom!

The French have been uncharacteristically unimaginative in the Christian names assigned their leaders. It was Charles twelve times, from Charlemagne to de Gaulle; and Louis eighteen. For the sake of historians and schoolchildren, they have all been given nicknames, to tell them apart.

Charles "The Hammer"
Pepin "The Short"
Charles "The Great," aka Charlemagne
Louis I "The Pious"
Charles I "The Bald"
Louis II "The Stammerer"
Louis III "The Weak"
Charles II "The Fat"
Charles III "The Simple"
Louis IV "Overseas"
Louis V "Do-Nothing," aka "The Sluggard"
Hugh "Capet" ("Of the Short Cape")
Robert II "The Pious," aka "The Wise"
Henry I
Philip I "The Amorous," aka "The Fair"
Louis VI "The Fat," aka "The Wide-Awake"
Louis VII "The Foolish"
Philip II "Augustus," aka "The Winker"
Louis VIII "Lionheart"
Louis IX "The Saint"
Philip III "The Bold"
Philip IV "The Fair"
Louis X "The Stubborn"
Philip V "The Tall"
Charles IV "The Fair," aka "The Bad"
Philip VI "The Trumped-Up"
John "The Good"
Charles V "The Wise"
Charles VI "The Foolish," aka "The Mad," "The Beloved"
Charles VII "The Well Served," aka "The Dauphin," "The Victorious"

Louis XI "The Universal Spider," aka "The Cruel"
Charles VIII "The Affable"
Louis XII "The Father of His People"
Francis I "The Great," aka "Father of Letters"
Henry II "The Warlike"[1]
Francis II[2]
Charles IX "The Foolish"
Henry III
Henry IV "The Great"
Louis XIII "The Just"
Louis XIV "The Grand Monarch," aka "The Sun King"
Louis XV "The Well Beloved"
Louis XVI "The Baker,"[3] aka "The Locksmith"
Napoleon Bonaparte[4] "The Nightmare of Europe," aka "The Little Corporal," "Corporal Violet," "The Man of Destiny," "Little Boney"
Louis XVIII "The King of Slops," aka "The Desired"
Charles X "Monsieur"
Louis-Philippe "The Citizen King," aka "Philippe Égalité," "Mr. Smith"
Louis Napoleon "The Man of Silence," aka "The Man of December," "The Man of Sedan"

Noble Experiments Department

ASSUMED TITLES

Titles are but nicknames, and every nickname is a title.
—Thomas Paine, *The Rights of Man*

Every man a king.
—Huey "Louisiana's Dictator" Long, aka "Kingfish"

KING OF THE MOONSHINERS   W. R. Gooch *distiller*
KING OF THE PIMPS   Charles "Lucky" Luciano *mobster*

1. It is to be noted that much Gallic irony applies to many of these titles. "Well Beloved," "Warlike," "Just," and "Desired," for example, were applied with heavy sarcasm.
2. Francis II had no nickname, but married Mary "Queen of Scots." He abdicated, and his brother Charles "The Foolish" distinguished himself by forthwith ordering the St. Bartholomew's Day Massacre. Two loyal sons of Catherine de Medici, Francis and Charles, were succeeded by their mother's favorite, Henry "The Male Milliner."
3. Marie Antoinette, "The Baker's Wife," was known to all as "Madame Deficit," as well as "The Austrian Baggage."
4. Between Louis "The Baker" and "Corporal Violet," France was more or less operated by Robespierre, "The Sea-Green Incorruptible."

KING OF THE UMPIRES   John Gaffney *baseball manager 1887*
KING OF THE LINKS   Bobby Jones *golfing great*
KING OF THE FAIRS   Carlos Figueroa *harness-horse trainer*
KING OF THE JOCKEYS, KING OF THE DERBIES   George Stern *jockey*
KING OF THE ROAD   Roger Miller *singer-songwriter*
KING OF BROADWAY   George M. Cohan *showman, Yankee Doodle Dandy*
KING OF THE ONE-LINERS   Henny Youngman *standup comic*
KING OF THE COWBOYS   Roy "The Singing Cowboy" Rogers (Leonard Slye) *actor*
   (see also "Queen of the Cowgirls," below)
KING OF COUNTRY MUSIC   Roy Acuff *musician, singer* / Hank Williams *song-writer-singer, aka "The Old Syrup-Sopper"* / etc.
KING OF WESTERN SWING   Bob Wills *fiddler, bandleader*
KING OF SWING   Benny "B. G." Goodman *jazz clarinetist, bandleader, aka "The Ray"*
KING OF JAZZ   Paul "Pops" Whiteman *bandleader*
KING OF THE HIGH C's   Luciano Pavarotti *opera star*
THE MARCH KING   John Phillip Sousa *composer-conductor*
WAYNE THE WALTZ KING   Wayne King *society bandleader*
THE SCHMALTZ KING   Guy Lombardo *bandleader, aka "Mr. New Year's Eve"*
THE AEROSOL KING   Robert Abplanalp *entrepreneur, aka "Nixon's Other Friend"*
   (see also "Bebe," Yayas)
THE ARTICHOKE KING, HAMBURGER KING, PINEAPPLE KING   (see Food)
THE JUNK BOND KING   Michael Milken *financier*
THE POLICY KING   Albert J. Adams *numbers man*
STANDARD OIL KING   John D. Rockefeller *stingy philanthropist*
KING ANDREW   (see "Old Hickory" Andy Jackson, U.S. Presidents)
KING PLEASURE   (Clarence Meeks) *jazz singer*
KING RADIO   Norman Span *announcer*
THE KING[1]   Elvis Presley *singer, legend, aka "The Pelvis," "The Memphis Flash," "The Hillbilly Cat"*
KING   Kingman Brewster *Yale prexy* / Nat Cole(s) *singer-pianist* / Curtis (Ousley) *sax great* / Clark Gable *movie idol* / Carl Hubbell *pitcher (see "Meal Ticket," Money)* / Michael Kelly *outfielder* / Larry "Nap" LaJoie *slugger-manager* / Battling Levinsky (see Assorted Mayhem) / Bill Linderman *rodeo rider* / (Joseph) Oliver *jazz band leader, cornet player* / Richard Petty *car racer*
THE UNCROWNED KING OF IRELAND   Charles Stewart Parnell *statesman*
THE UNCROWNED KING, THE PLUMED (or TATTOOED) KNIGHT   James G.

---

1. King. Elvis was managed by "Colonel" Tom Parker. The honorary military title was self-awarded by the Dutch-born Andreas Cornelius Kuijk. His real nickname was "Dries." Elvis called his beloved mother Gladys "Satnin." He called her toes "sooties." Elvis was called "E," "El," or "Elve" by "Sonny," "Red," and the other imaginative members of his entourage, which he called his "Memphis Mafia." Elvis called his penis "Little Elvis."

Blaine *secretary of state, aka "The Guano Statesman," "The Magnetic Man," "The Man from Maine"*

QUEEN OF THE COWGIRLS   Dale Evans (Frances Smith) *wife of "King of the Cowboys," above*

THE QUEEN OF CRIME   Agatha Christie *mystery writer*

THE QUEEN OF SOUL   Aretha Franklin *singer*

QUEEN OF THE VAMPIRES   (see "The Vamp," Love & Sex)

THE NIGHTCLUB QUEEN   Mary Louise Cecilia "Tex" Guinan *prohibition hostess*

QUEEN IDA   (Ida Lewis-Guillory) *zydeco musician, singer*

PRINCESS   Alice Roosevelt Longworth *Teddy's daughter*

THE PRINCE OF DARKNESS   Johnny Carson *late-night boob tube legend*

THE PRINCE OF HUMBUGS   P. T. Barnum *showman*

THE BLINTZ PRINCE, HOTCAKE BARON   etc. (see Food)

THE CLOWN PRINCE OF BASEBALL   Al Schacht *pitcher and showman*

THE CLOWN PRINCE OF BASKETBALL   Reese "Goose" Tatum *Harlem Globetrotter*

THE CROON PRINCE   Harry Lillis "Bing" Crosby *singer-actor, aka "Der Bingle," "The Great Groaner"*

THE PRINCE OF WAILS   Johnny Ray *emotive pop singer*

THE PRINCE OF WHALES   George IV *king of England, aka "The Fat Adonis"*

THE POLISH PRINCE   Pete "Stemmer" Stemkowski *hockey player* / Bobby Vinton *singer*

PRINCE ARTHUR   (see Chet "The Dude" Arthur, U.S. Presidents)

PRINCE BUSTER   (Roy Campbell) *reggae composer, performer*

PRINCE HAL   Harold Chase *crooked baseball great*

PRINCE   (Prince Rogers Nelson) *pop singer (see 100 One-Name Wonders)*

THE DUKE OF EARL   Gene Chandler *rock singer*

THE DUKE OF FLATBUSH   Edwin "Duke" Snider *Dodger outfielder*

THE DUKE OF MILWAUKEE   Al "Bucketfoot" Simmons *Braves outfielder*

THE DUKE OF TRALEE   Roger Bresnahan *Giants outfielder*

DUKE   Edward Kennedy Ellington *composer, pianist, bandleader* / Hugh "Losing Pitcher" Mulcahy / John Wayne (Marion Morrison) *actor*

IL DUCE   Benito Mussolini *aka "Muscle-ini," half the team of "Hit and Muss"*

DUCHESS   Mrs. Warren G. (Florence) Harding *first lady, aka "Boss"*

THE COUNT OF LUXEMBOURG   Henry "Heinie" Meine *pitcher*

COUNT NO COUNT   William Faulkner *Nobel prize–winning author*

COUNT   William Basie *pianist, bandleader* / Tony Mullane *pitcher, aka "The Apollo of the Box"*

LORD BUCKLEY   (Richard Buckley) *comedian, monologist*

LORD BYRON   Byron Nelson *golfing great*

LORD HAW HAW   William Joyce *British traitor, Nazi radio propagandist*

LORD HEE HAW   Frederick Kaltenbach *American traitor, Nazi radio propagandist*

LORD STIRLING   William Alexander *American Revolutionary general*

THE LAIRD OF SKIBO CASTLE   Andrew Carnegie *industrialist, philanthropist*
THE LAIRD OF WOODCHUCK LODGE   (see "John o' Birds," Birds)
LADY BIRD   Claudia Alta (Taylor) Johnson *LBJ's first lady*
LADY DAY   Billie Holiday (Eleanora Fagan) *blues singing immortal*
LADY LAZARUS   Judy Garland (Frances Gumm) *actress, singer*
LADY   Charles Baldwin *pitcher (won 42 games in 1886)*
THE EARL OF SNOHOMISH   Earl Averill *baseball Hall of Famer*
BARON CORVO   Frederick Rolfe *British author, eccentric*
SIR   Douglas Sahm *pop star* / Charles Thompson *"Bird" Parker's sideman*
SIR FRANCIS   Fran Tarkenton *Vikings quarterback, aka "Scramblin' Fran"*
SIR TIMOTHY   Tim Keefe *baseball Hall of Famer*
THE SQUIRE OF KENNET SQUARE   Herb Pennock *baseball Hall of Famer*
PHAROAH   Farell Sanders *jazz musician*
RAJAH   Rogers Hornsby *baseball legend*
SULTAN SALADIN   (Eugene Baldwin) *junior welterweight*
THE SULTAN OF SWAT   (see "Bambino," Age)
THE SHEIK   Rudolph Valentino (Rudolfo d'Antonguolla) *screen idol, aka "The Great Lover"*
THE KAISER   Franz Beckenbauer *German-born soccer star*
EMPRESS OF THE BLUES   Bessie Smith *singer*
THE CZAR OF BASEBALL   Kenesaw Mountain Landis *1st baseball commish*
THE CZAR OF THE UNDERWORLD   (see "Mr. Big," Size)
CZAR   Thomas B. "The Terrible Turk" Reed *Speaker of the House, aka "Biddy"*
ROYAL   Kazuo Kobayashi *junior featherweight champ 1976*
REBEL   Ennis Oakes, Thomas Olver *Dixie-born baseball players*
THE REBEL GIRL   Emma Goldman *anarchist organizer*
THE REBEL GOVERNOR   Jonathan Trumbull *Connecticut governor 1760–83*
WORLD B. FREE[2]   Lloyd Free *basketball star*
THE GREAT COMMONER   William Pitt "The Elder" *British statesman (see also "Silver-Tongue," Head to Toe [Mouths])*

---

2. World B. Free is no longer a nickname, since the irrepressible Lloyd has had it officially changed.

9

WHO'S ZOO

You cannot bear unless you are named for the bear. Bears can drive you crazy for saying their names.

—Kiowa Indian saying

A Man Called Horse Department

MAMMALS

BEAR   Paul Bryant *football coach* / Bob Hite *rock musician (Canned Heat)*
BIG UGLY BEAR   Charles "Sonny" Liston *heavyweight champ 1962–64*
THE BIG BEAR   Mike Garcia *pitcher*
LITTLE BEAR   Chester Zardis *jazz musician*
PAPA BEAR   George Halas *founder, head coach, "The Chicago Bears"*
THE GOLDEN BEAR   Jack Nicklaus *golfer, aka "Ohio Fats"*
HONEYBEAR   Eugene Sedric *sax player*
SUGARBEAR   Larvell Blanks *baseball player* / Randy Crowder *football player*
GRIZZLY   James Adams *frontiersman*
BEARCAT   John Overton Williams *jazz musician*
BEAR TRACKS   Al Javery, John Schmitz *baseball players*

THE ANIMAL   Ken Bannister *basketball player* / Dick Butkus *football player* / Frank Fletcher *fighter*
ANIMAL   Eddie Lopez *heavyweight challenger 1980*
THE BEAST   Benjamin Butler *Union general, aka "Spoons"* / Frank Falanga *mobster* / Jimmy "Double X" Foxx *baseball Hall of Famer*
THE GREAT BEAST[1]   Edward "Alistair" Crowley *diabolist*

1. The Great Beast. Crowley, who dabbled in the dark arts and wrote silly books, claimed to be the "Great Beast" foretold in the Book of Revelations. To prove how wicked he was, he ate his own sperm. Wow!

WHALE   Fred Walters *baseball player*

BABY WHALE[2]   Dave "The Cobra" Parker *baseball player*

GORILLA   William Jones *middleweight champ 1931–32*

THE GORILLA WOMAN   Dian Fossey *anthropologist*

RING GORILLA   Phil Bloom *fighter*

BABOON, THE ILLINOIS APE, THE ORIGINAL GORILLA   Abraham Lincoln (see "Honest Abe" Lincoln, U.S. Presidents)

MONKEY   Pete Hotaling *baseball player*

THE MONKEY MAN   John T. Scopes *biology teacher*

APEMAN MUDGEON   (see "Volcano Jones," Weather)

MONKEY WARD   Montgomery Ward Co. *(compare "Sawbuck")*

RHINO   Homer Jones *football player*

RYNO   Ryne Sandberg *Cubs infielder*

THE LION   William Henry Joseph Benthol Bonaparte Berthloff "Willie" Smith *jazz pianist*

LITTLE LION   Alexander Hamilton *founding father, "Alexander the Coppersmith"*

LONE LION, THE IDAHO LION   William E. "The Big Potato" Borah *senator*

TIGER   Theo "The Georgia Deacon" Flowers *middleweight champ 1926* / Ralph Williams *hockey goon*

TIGER MANN   (Kusak Kameniak) *fighter*

THE TAMMANY TIGER   William "Boss" Tweed *NYC politician, "Big Bill"*

PUMA   Sandra Jones *backup singer*

JOHN COUGAR[3]   (John Mellencamp) *pop singer*

THE MICHIGAN WILDCAT   Ad Wolgast *lightweight champ 1910–12*

THE CAMEL   Murray Humphreys *gangster*

KANGAROO   Billy Cunningham, Donald Smith *basketball players*

KANGAROOSEVELT   (see Franklin "Boss" Roosevelt, U.S. Presidents)

MOOSE[4]   Bob Lee *pitcher, aka "Horse"* / Bill Skowron *baseball player* / Elmer Vasko *hockey player*

BIG MOOSE   Johnny Walker *bluesman* / Edward "Big Ed" Walsh *baseball player*

BULL MOOSE   Benjamin Jackson *blues singer (recorded "I Want a Bow-Legged Woman")* / Teddy Roosevelt (see U.S. Presidents)

BULL   William Burroughs *novelist, aka Bill Lee* / William F. Halsey *U.S. admiral* / Greg Luzinski *baseball slugger*

2. Baby Whale. Pitcher Bill "Spaceman" Lee hung this tag on slugger "Cobra" Parker when the latter appeared grossly overweight. Parker later blamed his condition on a cocaine habit—which drug is not usually considered an appetite stimulant.

3. John Cougar, when being fobbed off as a sexy rocker, took the "Cougar" tag. Now being fobbed off as a sensitive folkie, he has reverted to his original name.

4. Moose. Bill Skowron, New York Yankee first baseman, was not named for the animal he nearly resembled as an adult, but for "Moose-olini" the Italian dictator he allegedly resembled as a child.

THE BULL   Jerry Martin *fighter*
BABY BULL   Orlando "Cha Cha" Cepeda *baseball player*
THE BRONX BULL   Jacob "Jake" LaMotta *middleweight champ 1949–51*
THE WILD BULL OF THE PAMPAS   Luis Angel Firpo *heavyweight challenger*
COW COW   Charles Davenport *jazz pianist*
OX   Frank Pennie *football player* / St. Thomas Aquinas *theologian*
BUFFALO[5]   Charles Jones *wildlife exterminator, ecologist*
BUFFALO BILL   William Frederick "Wild Bill" Cody *scout, showman, aka "The Messenger"*
THE WILD ELK OF THE WASATCH   Ed Heusser *baseball player*
REINDEER   Bill Killefer *baseball umpire*
THE ANTELOPE   Emil Verban *baseball player*
THE EBONY ANTELOPE   Jesse Owens *track star, aka "The Ebony Express"*
DEERFOOT   Harry Bay *baseball player*
THE HORSE   Alan Ameche *Colts football back*
HARRY THE HORSE   Harry Danning *baseball player*
THE IRON HORSE   Lou Gehrig (see "The Durable Dutchman," Them)
LIGHT-HORSE HARRY   Henry Lee *U.S. cavalry general*
RACEHORSE   Lamar Davis *baseball player* / A. B. Williams *theatrical producer*
WAR HORSE   James W. A. Nicholson *Union naval officer*
WILD HORSE   Neill Sheridan *baseball player*
HORSE BELLY   Joe Sargent *baseball player*
CRAZY HORSE   Tim Foli *baseball player*
OL' HOSS   Charles Radbourn *baseball Hall of Famer*
THE WILD HOSS OF THE OSAGE   Johnny "Pepper" Martin *St. Louis baseball star, "Gas House Gang" member*
BRONCO BILLY   Gilbert M. Anderson (Max Aronson) *filmmaker*
BRONKO   Bronislaw Nagurski *football running back*
PONY   Norwood Poindexter *sax player*
WHOA   Bill Phillips *baseball player*
MULE   Perry Bradford *pianist* / George Haas *baseball player*
MULEY   Robert "Farmer Bob" Doughton *North Carolina politician*
THE DESERT FOX   Erwin Rommel *German general*
THE SILVER FOX   Charlie Rich *country singer*
OLD FOX   Clark Griffith *baseball owner-manager* / George Washington (see U.S. Presidents)
REDD FOXX   (John Sanford) *actor, comedian*
SWAMP FOX   Francis Marion *American Revolutionary commander*
WOLFIE   Jim Wohlford *baseball player*
HOWLIN' WOLF   (Chester Arthur Burnett) *blues singer, guitarist*

5. Buffalo. Hunter Charles Jones once claimed the world record for bison slaughter; then, when the creatures were near extinction, he became a millionaire as rancher of same.

THE SHE-WOLF   Mary Todd Lincoln *first lady*
CARLOS THE JACKAL   Ilyich Ramirez-Sanchez *failed assassin*
RAM   Roger Ramirez *jazz pianist*
THE LAMB   Edgar Sampson *sax player*
GOAT   Harry Anderson *error-prone baseball star*
GOAT GLAND[6]   John R. Brinkley *health faddist, con man*
HOG   Richard III *king of England, aka "Crookback"*
PIG   Frank House *baseball player*
PIGGY   Frank Ward *baseball player* / Ward L. Lambert *football coach*
THE POSSUM   George Jones *country singer*
POSSUM   Earl Whitted *baseball player*
CHINCHILLA   Sergey Diaghilev *Russian ballet producer, art critic*
THE MOLE   James Earl Ray *assassin, alias Eric Starve Galt*
PETER PORCUPINE   *pseudonym of William Cobbett, writer, pamphleteer*
SKUNK   Jeff Baxter *rock sideman* / Daryl Sanders *football player*
THE WEASEL   Don Bessent *baseball player* / Van Buren (see U.S. Presidents)
THE OLD MONGOOSE   Archie "Old Man River" Moore *light heavyweight champ*
MONGOOSE   Eddie Lukon *baseball player*
THE BEAVER[7]   Max Aiken, Lord Beaverbrook *publisher* / Simone de Beauvoir *writer*
BEAVER   Russell Blinco *hockey player*
LITTLE BEAVER   Frank Rowe *rodeo rider*
BEAVER PELT   Bruce Emmerson *rodeo rider*
MUSKRAT   Bill Shipke *baseball player*
SEA LION   Charlie Hall *pitcher*
THE SEATTLE SEAL   Jack Medica *swimmer*
SQUIRREL   Roy Sievers *baseball player*
SQUIRREL HEAD   George B. Terrell *Texas politician*
CHIP MONCK   (Edward Bersford Monck) *rock impresario*
RABBIT   Walter Maranville *baseball Hall of Famer*
THE RABBIT   Johnny Hodges *soprano sax player*
JACKRABBIT   Jim Abbitt *football player*
BLACK RABBIT   Billy Ray Smith *football player*
BUNNY   Rowland Berrigan *trumpeter* / Edmund Wilson *dean of critics*

6. Goat Gland. A Kansas quack with a vast radio following during the depression, Brinkley diagnosed illnesses and prescribed his own patent mail-order medicines over the air, and made $12 million doing it. He rose to prominence by allegedly restoring the virility of customers by transplanting bits of goat gland into their depressed testicles.

7. The Beaver. Max Aiken, Canadian-born English publishing mogul, chose the patriotic "Beaverbrook" as his title when raised to the peerage—the aquatic rodent in question being the Canadian national animal. One assumes Simone got the name in tribute to her hard work, not as a slur on *The Second Sex*.

BUNNY WAILER   (Neville Livingston) *reggae musician*
MOUSE   Alvin Burroughs *drummer* / Irving Randolph *trumpeter*
THE MOUSE   Bruce Strauss *fighter*
MICKEY MOUSE   (see Cartoon & Other Literary Figures)
MOUSIE   Walter Blum *jockey*
THE RAT   Kenny Linseman *hockey player*
THE WHITE RAT   Dorrel "Whitey" Herzog *baseball manager*
SWAMP RAT   Don "Big Daddy" Garlitz *car racer*

The Dog House Department

CANINES

DOG MAN   Arthur Jackson *drummer*
DOGGIE   George Miller *baseball player, aka "Calliope," "Foghorn"*
BIG DOG   Ernest A. Nevers *football player, coach*
BIRD DOG   Bill Hopper *pitcher*
BULLDOG   Jim Bouton *pitcher* / Benjamin Franklin Cheatham *U.S. major general* / Henry Patterson *fighter* / Clyde Turner *football player*
DARWIN'S BULLDOG   (see "Episcophagous," Religion & Mystery)
THE TOY BULLDOG   Edward "Mickey" Walker *middleweight champ 1926–31*
MAD DOG   Vincent Coll *killer* / Jack O' Billovich *football player* / Danny Paul *fighter*
MOONDOG   (Louis Thomas Hardin) *composer*
OLD DOG   Louis Ritter *catcher*
RED DOG   Edward Dougherty *rodeo rider*
SKYDOG   Duane Allman *the guitarist's nickname on a William Royce "Boz" Scaggs album*
3 DOG   Willie Davis *baseball player*
HOUND DOG   Theodore Taylor *musician* / Rufus Thomas *singer*
THE HOUND   Bob Kelly *hockey player*
BLOODHOUND   Sir Archibald Wavell *British general*
POODLES   Edwin Hanneford *circus clown* / Joe Hutheson *baseball player*
MUTT   Johnny Riddle *baseball player*
PAPA MUTT   Thomas Carey *trumpet player*
POOCH   Clyde Barnhart *baseball player*
BOWSER   (John Baumann) *singer*
FIDO   Herbert Kempton *ivy league football player*
SPOT   Chet Falk *baseball player* / Arthur Potts *British cartoonist (pseudonym)*
DOG CHOW JACK   John Danforth *Missouri senator, Ralston Purina heir*
BOW WOW   Hank Arft *baseball player*

The Cat House Department

FELINES

CAT   William Anderson *jazz trumpeter* / B. Holt Milner *minor league baseball player* / Gogen Yamaguchi *karate instructor*

THE CAT   Harry Brecheen *baseball player*

CAT STEVENS   (Stephen Georgiou) *singer*

BIG CAT   Johnny Mize *baseball Hall of Famer*

THE HILLBILLY CAT   Elvis Presley (see "The King," Assumed Titles)

THE LONE CAT   Jesse Fuller *one-man band*

TOP CAT   Cubby Jackson *jazz musician*

KITTEN   Harvey Haddix *baseball manager (of "Harvey's Wall Bangers")*

THE SEX KITTEN   Brigitte Bardot (Camille Javal) *actress*

KITTY   Katherine Hart Carlisle *celebrity*

PUSSY   Charles A. Tebeau *baseball player* / Alice B. Toklas *(to Gertrude "Lovely" Stein)*

PUSSY FOOT   William Eugene Johnson *G-man, "Untouchable"*

GATO   Leandro Barbieri *musician*

MEOW   Len Gilmore *baseball player*

Fine Feathered Friends Department

BIRDS

BIRD, YARDBIRD   Charlie Parker *sax great (in the South, "yardbird" means chicken)*

LADY BIRD   Claudia Alta Johnson *first lady, Linda Bird's mom*

BIG BIRD   Mark "The Bird" Fidrych *baseball player*

LOVEBIRD   William F. Allen *politician*

INDIANA'S SONGBIRD   Helen Bucher *entertainer*

THE BIRDMAN OF ALCATRAZ   Robert Franklin Stroud *inmate, caged on "The Rock"*

BIRDIE   George Tebbetts *baseball manager*

JOHN O' BIRDS, GRAY-CRESTED FLY-CATCHER   John Burroughs *naturalist, aka "The Laird of Woodchuck Lodge"*

CHICKEN, DUCK, GOOSE, TURKEY (see Food)

THE GAME CHICKEN   Henry "Hen" Pearce *heavyweight champ 1803–06*

ATTILA THE HEN   Margaret "Milk Snatcher" Thatcher *British PM, aka "The Iron Maiden"*

ROOSTER BEN   Ben Webster *sax great*

THE RED ROOSTER   Doug "Rojo" Rader *3rd baseman, manager*

THE GREAT THUNDERING ROOSTER[1]   U.S. "Crackdown" Johnson
BANTAM   Ben "The Ice Man" Hogan *golfer*
CHICK   Charles Hafey *baseball player* / William Webb *drummer*
THE SINGING CAPON   Nelson Eddy *singer*
TONY DUCKS   Anthony Corallo *crime boss*
DONALD DUCK   (see Cartoon & Other Literary Figures)
MAD DUCK   Alex Karras *football player, actor*
DUCKY SWANN   Henry Swann *baseball player*
DUCKY WUCKY   Joe "Muscles" Medwick *baseball player*
GANDER   Monty Stratton *pitcher*
TURKEYFOOT   Frank Brower *baseball player*
THE AUK   Sir Claude Auchinleck *British general*
DR. BUZZARD   (see Doctors)
COOT   Orville Veal *baseball player*
CRANE   Frank Reberger *baseball player*
CROW   Warren Cromartie, Frank Crosetti *baseball players*
CUCKOO   Walter "Seacap" Christensen *baseball player*
DODO   Michael Marmarosa *musician*
DODO BIRD   Frank Bird *baseball player*
AGED EAGLE   T. S. Eliot *poet, dramatist, aka "Old Possum"*
BALD EAGLE   Y. A. "Ya Ya" Tittle *quarterback*
FLAPPING EAGLE   Lionel Harney *fighter*
THE BLACK EAGLE OF HARLEM[2]   Col. Hubert F. Julian *mercenary*
THE GREY EAGLE   Tristam "Tris" Speaker *baseball Hall of Famer, aka "Spoke"*
THE LONE EAGLE   Charles "Lucky Lindy" Lindbergh *aviator hero*
THE EAGLE ORATOR OF SOUTH CAROLINA   John C. Calhoun *statesman*
THE HAWK   Kid Gavilan (Geraldo Gonzalez) *welterweight champ 1951–54*
HAWK[3]   Ken Harrelson *Bosox infielder*
BATTLE HAWK   Kujoshi Kazama *junior lightweight contender 1980*
THE ARKANSAS HUMMINGBIRD   Lon Warnecke *C&W singer*
JAYBIRD (JAILBIRD)   Burl Coleman *blues harmonica player*
MEADOWLARK   George Lemon *Harlem Globetrotter*
THE SWEDISH NIGHTINGALE   Jenny Lind *turn-of-the-century soprano superstar*
THE OWL   Basil Banghart *burglar* / Jack Garner (see "Poker Face," Head to Toe
   [Faces]) / Burt "Hootie" Hooton *pitcher*

1. Great Thundering Rooster. Feisty Brigadier General Hugh J. Johnson, given charge of the National Recovery Administration by FDR, was also known as "Ironpants," a name he had acquired as a cavalry officer.
2. The Black Eagle of Harlem. Julian was an eccentric aviator, who volunteered to defend Abyssinia against the Italian Fascist invaders, thus becoming commanding officer and only member of Ethiopia's air force.
3. Hawk. Many ballplayers are called "Hawk" because of their fielding abilities. Harrelson could snag liners with the best, but got the name for his profile.

PARTRIDGE   George Adams *Syracuse outfielder 1879*
PUFFIN   Herbert Henry Asquith *British statesman*
SNIPE   Roy Hansen *Phillies pitcher 1930–35*
SPARROW   William Morton *pitcher*
THE LITTLE SPARROW   Edith Piaf *chanteuse*
THE STORK LADY   Georgene Faulkner *radio storyteller*
THE MAD STORK   Ted Hendricks *football end*
THE DIXIE THRUSH   Sammy Strang *Giants, Dodgers infielder*
THE VULTURE   Phil Regan *Tigers, Dodgers relief pitcher*
VULTURE VINCHELL   Walter Winchell (see "Little Beau Peep," Cartoon & Other
   Literary Figures)
BIRD CAGE   Lew Burdette *pitcher*
BIRD EYE   Harry Truby *2nd baseman 1895*
BIRD LEGS   Willie Jensen *U.S. flyweight champ 1970*
PECK   Mancy Carr *banjo player*
THE GUANO STATESMAN   (see "The Uncrowned King," Assumed Titles)
TWEET   Joe Walsh *Braves shortstop 1938*

In Cold Blood Department

REPTILES, AMPHIBIANS & FISH

DINOSAUR   Jim Jensen *scientist*
PTERODACTYL   Charlie Kerfeld *pitcher*
COBRA   Dave Parker *baseball slugger*
THE CINCINNATI COBRA   Ezzard Charles *heavyweight champ 1949–51*
THE MOTOR CITY COBRA   Thomas "Hitman" Hearns *fighter*
THE SMILING COBRA   James T. Aubrey, Jr. *network exec*
THE SMILING PYTHON   Dick Walsh *baseball player*
SNAKE   Knowlton Ames, Kenny Stabler *football players*
THE SNAKE   Ruby Ortiz *fighter* / Don Prudhomme *car racer*
JAKE THE SNAKE   Jacques Plante *hockey goaltender*
SNAKEHEAD, SNAKEHIPS   (see Head to Toe)
THE CROCODILE   Averell "Honest Ave" Harriman *diplomat, politician*
GATOR   Ron "Louisiana Lightning" Guidry *pitcher*
GATOR TAIL   Willis Jackson *jazz musician*
SNAPPING TURTLE   George Carter Glass *politician*
NEWT   Fred Hunter *baseball player*
FROG   Lester "Smiley" Burnette *cowboy actor*
BULLFROG   Bill Dietrich *pitcher*
FROGGY   Billy Laughlin *actor (Our Gang)* / James Williams *football player*
FROGMAN   Clarence Henry *musician*

HOP TOAD   Guiseppe Giunta *hitman*
THE WORM   Willie McCarter *basketball player* / Willie Monroe *fighter*
SLUG   Harry Heilmann *baseball Hall of Famer*
FISHY   Phil Rabinowitz *basketball player*
CAPTAIN SHRIMP   Myles Standish *colonist*
BIG SHRIMP   Allie Sherman *Giants football coach*
BIG TUNA   Anthony Accardo *criminal*
CATFISH[1]   Jim Hunter *pitcher*
COD   Albert Myers *baseball player*
THE CRAB   Jesse Burkett *baseball Hall of Famer*
THE EBONY EEL   Aze Simmons *football player*
SMOKE HERRING   Bill Herring *baseball player*
KINGFISH   Huey P. Long (see Assumed Titles)
MUDCAT   Jim Grant *baseball player*
THE OCTOPUS   Martin Marion *baseball player*
OYSTER   Thomas P. Burns *baseball player*
PIKE   Clifton Davis *trumpeter*
MIKE DE PIKE   Mike Heitler *criminal*
RAINBOW TROUT   Steve Trout *pitcher, son of "Dizzy"*
SHAD   Lester Collins *trumpeter* / Charles Rhem, Clay Roe *baseball players*
THE WHITE SHARK   Greg Norman *golfer*
SHARKEY   Joe Bonano *trumpeter*
JACK SHARKEY   (Joseph Paul Cukoschay) *heavyweight champ 1932–33, aka "The Boston Gob," "The Fighting Fool"*
SNAPPER   (Robert) Ford Garrison *baseball player*
SQUIDLY   Sid Fernandez *baseball player*
BARNACLE BILL   Bill Sutphin *New Jersey politician*
FISH BAIT, ALLIGATOR BAIT   William B. Miller *Senate employee*
FISH HOOK   Allyn Stout *baseball player*
THE MAD MACKEREL MERCHANT   (see Professions)

The Bug House Department

INSECTS

THE BUG   Meyer Lansky *criminal, alias "Johnny Eggs"*
BUG   James Holliday *baseball player*
BUGS   John Hamilton *drummer* / George Moran *Chicago gang leader*

1. Catfish. This colorful nickname was given pitcher Hunter by Charles O. Finley, then owner of the Oakland Athletics, for whom Catfish toiled. "Charlie O" believed ballplayers should have snappy names. He dubbed pitcher Johnny Lee Odom "Blue Moon," but couldn't even bribe Vida Blue to call himself "True" Blue.

GOLD BUG   Thomas Hart Benton *Missouri senator, aka "Old Bullion," "Old Humbug"*

JUNE BUG   Vernon Perry *football player*

KISSING BUG   Richard Hobson *naval hero*

BUGSY   Benjamin Siegel *gangster*

ANTS   Walter Atanas *hockey player*

ADAM ANT   (Stuart Goddard) *pop singer*

BEE   Edward W. Houston *guitarist* / Bertha Walker *American composer*

B. BUMBLE   (Jack Fina) *musician (of B. Bumble and the Stingers)*

BEETLE   Walter Smith *U.S. Army officer, WWI, aka "Bulldog"*

BEETLES   Robert S. Bailey *baseball player*

BO-WEAVIL   James Jackson *blues musician*

BUTTERFLY   Steve Hughes *fighter* / Thelma McQueen *actress*

THE IRON BUTTERFLY   Imelda Marcos *wife of former dictator Ferdinand*

THE LOUSE   Mickey Cohen *gangster*

FLEA   Herman Clifton, Bob Lillis *baseball players*

THE FLEA   Freddie "Moochie" Patek *shortstop*

FLY   Steve Mingori *baseball player*

THE FLY   Richard Rozelle *fighter*

GRASSHOPPER   Jim Lillie *baseball player*

THE CRICKET   Billy Rigney *baseball manager, aka "Specs"*

THE GREEN HORNET   Gen. George S. Patton *aka "Flash Gordon," "Old Blood and Guts," "The Old Man"*

THE MIGHTY MITE, FLEA   Miller "Hug" Huggins *baseball player*

THE MIGHTY MITE   "Little Albie" Booth *football player, aka "Little Boy Blue"*

SKEETER DAVIS   (Mary Francis Penick) *country singer*

THE HARLEM SPIDER   Tommy "Spider" Kelly *fighter*

SPIDER   John Koerner *blues guitarist* / Carl Lockhart *football player* / Johnny Newman *basketball player* / Emile Pladner *fighter* / Vladimir Sabich *slain skier* / Travis Webb *car racer*

SPYDER   Dwight Turner *singer*

THE UNIVERSAL SPIDER   Louis XIV *French king, reigned 1643–1715*

BLACK WIDOW   Milton Owens *fighter*

DADDY LONG LEGS   Bill McAdoo *secretary of the treasury, aka "Dancing Fool"*

TERMITE   Maurice Watkins *fighter*

TICK   Thomas Gray *jazz trumpeter*

COOTIE   Charles Williams *jazz trumpeter*

BUZZ   (see Ringers)

STING   (Gordon Sumner) *British pop singer*

THE SULTAN OF SWAT   (see "Bambino," Age)

10
GRAVE MATTERS

Nickname, Sickname Department

DISEASES

Diseases are not named, lest they come upon the namer. Leprosy, for instance, is mentioned in Arabia as "the blessed disease."
— Standard Dictionary of Folklore

Doctors call it iron deficiency anemia. We call it "tired blood."
— tiresome TV commercial

Maybe it's because the "real" names for diseases are in Latin, the ritual witch-doctor mumbo jumbo of the medieval profession. Maybe it's because the "real" names are so *icky*. Maybe it's a deep-seated taboo. For whatever reason, we give our medical problems nicknames, and apply the same nicknaming techniques to them as we do with our friends . . .

Euphemisms

"The Kissing Disease" (mononucleosis) can lead to "cold sores" (herpes labialis), "brides' disease" (urethritis), and/or "clap," "ladies' fever," "French pox," "gleet," "morning drop" (gonorrhea) . . . even, these days, "AIDS," the kind-of-cute acronym-nickname for the dreadful acquired immune deficiency syndrome.

Initials

Jerry's kids have MD. Others have MS. Poets get TB and sometimes the DTs. Everybody gets the Big C.

Associations

As with ordinary folks, diseases acquire their nicknames from connections with celebrities, occupations, and places:

"Lou Gehrig's disease" = amyotrophic lateral sclerosis
"farmers' lung" = granulomatous
"Rocky Mountain spotted fever" = rickettsiosis
"Mexican quickstep" ("Montezuma's revenge") = diarrhea
"German measles" = rubella
"bricklayer's anemia" = ancylostomiasis
"athlete's foot" = tinea pedis
"tailor's bottom" = bursitis
"baker's leg" = genu varum
"teacher's nodes" = chorditis tuberosa
"swimmer's ear" = external otitis
"nailer's consumption" = siderosis
"ragpicker's disease" = anthrax
"the king's evil" = scrofula
"the royal disease" = hemophilia
"St. Vitus' dance" = rheumatic chorea
"St. Anthony's fire" = erysipelas

Abbreviations/Diminutives

Some illnesses actually get *pet names:*

"polio" = poliomyelitis
"dip" = diphtheria

"flu" = viral influenza
"syph" = syphilis

Then there are pluralized diminutives (think of people called Moms, Pops, Slats, or Fats . . .). So:

"rattles" = angina
"zits" = acne
"heaves" = asthma
"bends" = caisson disease
"yaws" = frambesia
"rabies" = hydrophobia
"scabies" = sarcoptic acariasis
"trots," "runs," "lurkies," and
  "Hershey squirts" = diarrhea

"jerks" = rheumatic chorea
"crimps" = rheumatism
"mumps" = parotitis
"measles" = rubeola
"hives" = uriticaria
"chilblains" = pernio
"pins and needles" = acroparaesthesia

Often diseases, like one's pals and home teams, are nicknamed by a distinguishing color:

"black death" = bubonic plague
"black eye" = circumorbital hematoma

"black lung" = pneumoconiosis
"blue baby" = cyanosis

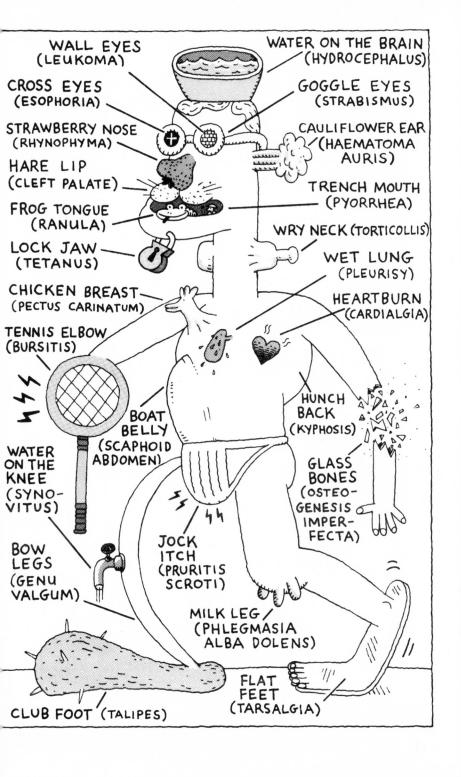

"blue balls" = gonorrhea
"blue bloater" = chronic bronchitis
"brown lung" = byssinosis
"green sickness" = chlorosis
"pink eye" = conjunctivitis
"pink puffer" = emphysema
"red measles" = rubeola

"red soldier" = " hog chorea
"scarlet fever" = scarlatina
"white lung" = asbestiosis
"white plague" = tuberculosis
"the whites" = leukorrhea
"yellow fever" also called "yellow jack"

The word "fever" is for some reason a preferred component of disease nicknames. So:

"hay fever" = allergic rhinitis
"valley fever" = coccidioidomycosis
"cabin fever" = claustrophobia
"breakbone fever," "bucket fever," "dandy fever" = dengue
"swamp fever" = malaria
"spring fever" = melancholia
"winter fever" = pneumonia
"trench fever" = quintan
"rabbit fever" = tularemia
"jail fever" = typhus

There are even a few animal disease nicknames (as you might expect), including "rabbit fever" (above), "chicken pox" (varicella), and "pink elephants" (delirium tremens) . . . And some "action-descriptions" too: "galloping consumption" is tuberculosis, "whooping cough" is pertussis, and "walking pneumonia" is mycoplasm.

What in God's Name Department

UPSTAIRS

In Homeric times, people and things had two names: the one given them by men and the one given by the gods. I wonder what God calls me.
—Miguel de Unamuno

The ancient Greeks believed themselves to be at the mercy of cruel and vengeful spirits, the Furies. Whenever they spoke of them, they called them *Eumenides,* "The Kindly Ones." The country folk of Ireland are similarly plagued and tormented by wicked spirits (no, not the English)—and are careful always to speak of them as "The Good People," "The Little People," "The Fair Folk."

The Hebrews of Old Testament times were forbidden to utter the name·

of their deity, *Yahweh*. His name was "ineffable," unspeakable . . . indeed, it could only be *written* in a kind of code: the tetragrammaton YHWH ("Yad-hay-vav-hay"). The King James Bible's "Jehova," by the way, is the error of a transcribing monk back in 1516.

But the Jews thought about, and talked and wrote about, their God constantly. To do so, they came up with many nicknames for him. The Kebala, a medieval mystical Hebrew text, lists seventy-two nicknames of God. Among them are: *Adonai* (strangely, for monotheists, a plural, meaning "My Lords"); *Elohim* (another plural, meaning "gods"); *Attik Yomin* (the "Ancient of Days"); *ha Shem* ("the Name"); *Yah* (a simple abbreviation); as well as: *Etrha, Agla, Aleph, Eyeh, Ejel, Asser, Agios, Adiriron, En Sof, Shaddai, Elyon, Kedosh, Shekhina, Zohar-ariel, Akh-ariel, ha Gevurah* . . . that's twenty-one.

To list them all, the Christian alchemists believed, was to cause something wonderful—and fearful—to happen. (In far-off Tibet, even now, Buddhist monks are writing down, on little pieces of paper, one by one, the million names of God. When they finish, the world will end.)

The Jewish prohibition against speaking the Divine Name persisted, in Christendom, until recently. (Now that we're all agnostics, we say "Oh, my Gawd!" all the time.) Whatever happened to: "Gads," "Gar," "Godfrey," "Gol," "Golly," "Gosh," and "by Gum"? Or "Law," "Lawdie," "Lawzie," and "Lordy," for land's sake? "The Almighty," "The Creator," "The Divinity," the "First Cause," "The Lord," "Providence," or the "Supreme Being," for goodness' sake? Or, more familiarly, "The Great Scorer," "The Big Guy," "The Topside Joss Man," "The Man Upstairs"? Jumpin' Jee-hosaphat!

The "Son of God" (one of the nicknames He gave Himself—"Son of Man" was another) was born Yeshua ben David. "Jesus" is an approximation of the very old Hebrew name. "Christ" is, if not exactly a nickname, a diminutive of the Greek sobriquet *Christos,* which is a translation of the Hebrew term for "Annointed One," "Messiah."

These days, He's "Our Lord," "The Good Shepherd," "The Sacred Heart," "The Lamb of God," "Gee-Zoz" (according to TV evangelists), "Jeez," "Gee" "Gee-whiz," "Judas Priest," "Cripes," and "Cryin' Out Loud." His original disciples addressed Him as "Lord," "Master," and "Rabbi." It was Pontius Pilate who assigned to Him the mocking title "King of the Jews."

As for the apostles themselves, like an outlaw band, fraternity, or platoon, they called each other (and are known to us) by nicknames. Simon ben Jona got his witty tag from The Master himself (who on other occasions addressed the First Pope as "Satan"). Jesus gave Simon the name "Petros," a pun on the Greek word for rock. We know him as Peter, but "Rocky" might be a better translation.

We don't know Rocky's kid brother's original Hebrew name. We call him by his Greek tag, "Andrew," which means, roughly "Macho."

Jesus called the hot-tempered brothers James and John "The Sons of Thunder."

John (really Jokanon) was also "The Beloved," with implications of "Teacher's Pet." John's brother James we know as James "The Greater" (bigger, older), to distinguish him from James "The Lesser." "Lesser" means "young" as well as "short." They're Big Jimbo and Little Jimmy . . .

Matthew ("God's gift") changed his name from Levi.

There being a John already, the other John took a Latin name, Mark. The other Simon, meanwhile, got the sobriquet "The Zealot." When Joseph joined up, he assumed the name "Son of Consolation," that is, Barnabus. Newcomer Bartholomew became Nathaniel. Last to join was Saul of Tarsus, who, with uncharacteristic humility, assumed the name Paul, from the Latin word for "little," *paulus*. Call Paul "Tiny."

The disciple known to the others as "The Twin" has come down to us with the most famous sobriquet of all: "Doubting Thomas."

Speak of the Devil Department

DOWNSTAIRS

"Speak of the Devil and he will appear," as everyone knows. That is, if we call him by his proper name (or names), we will conjure up an evil spirit. To avoid doing so, we've been singularly creative in thinking up synonyms—nicknames—for the Devil . . . lest the smell of brimstone assault our nostrils and a dreadful voice be heard to say, "Pleased to meet you, hope you've guessed my name!"

"The Adversary" (somewhat legalistic)
"Auld Clootie" (popular in Scotland)
"The Deuce" (as in "What the deuce?")
"The Demon" (actually, there are lots of demons, each with his own name)
"The Destroyer"
"The Dickens" (not a reference to 19th-century author Charles—"Dickens" for
    Devil is in Shakespeare)
"The Dragon" (so he is portrayed with St. Michael defeating him)
"The Evil One" (cruel, but accurate)
"The Father of Lies" (so Christ called him)
"The Fiend" (or "Foul Fiend")

"His Satanic Majesty" (honorific)

"Legion" (so he told Christ his name was)

"Lucifer" (the angel who rebelled in heaven and was cast out)

"Lord of the Flies" (a translation of the Hebrew *Beelzebub*)

"Moloch" (a "false" god, worshipped by Israel's neighbors)

"The Old One," "Old Gentleman," "Old Enemy," "Old Bendy," "Old Gooseberry,"
"Old Harry," "Old Horny" (when identified with the pagan nature spirit Pan,
whence his horns and cloven hoofs), "Old Ned," "Old Nick," "Old Scratch"
(popular in New Hampshire—but from the Old Norse *scrach,* meaning goblin).

"The Prince of Darkness"

"The Prince of the Powers of the Air"

"Roundfoot"

"Sam Hill" (from the old West—an outlaw's name that punned on hell?)

"Satan" (a Persian word, identifying him with Darkness [evil] as opposed to Light
[good] in their scheme of things. *Iran* is Persian for "Light"—so when Ayatollah
Khomeini called Jimmy Carter "That Great Satan," he just meant "anti-Ira-
nian."

"Screwface" (Jamaican slang)

"The Serpent" (from his first appearance in the Bible, as a walking, talking, and
most beautiful creature)

"The Tempter" (a classic "occupational" nickname)

Religions—that is, other people's religions—get nicknames, too.
"Goyim," "Infidel," "Heathen," "Pagan," and "Cult Member" come to mind
. . . In America, freedom is constitutionally guaranteed to: "Dunkers" (the
Church of the Brethren, who baptize by total immersion), "Hard Shell
Baptists" ("primitive," unreconstructed Southern Baptists); "Holy Rollers"
(the Church of God, wherein members allegedly roll on the floor), "Hooks
and Eyes" (the Amish, a puritan sect who do not practice buttoning),
"Mackerel Snappers" (Roman Catholics, who once ate fish on Fridays),
"Moonies" (the Unification Church, founded by Sun Myung Moon), "Mor-
mons" (the Latter-Day Saints, for their founding angel's name), "Papists"
(see "Mackerel Snappers"), "Presbos" (Presbyterians), "Quakers" (the Society of Friends, who are enjoined to quake with Fear of the Lord), "Sally
Ann" (the Salvation Army, in hobo lingo), and "Shakers" (the United Society of Believers), furniture stylists, and once a puritan sect who "shook,"
that is, danced enthusiastically, in order to sublimate sexual desire. It
worked. There are no Shakers left.

And of course there are "Jesus Freaks," "Bluenoses," "Bible Punchers,"
"Snake Handlers," and a variety of slurs on Protestant sects.

Jews are generally slandered ethnically rather than by religious persua-
sion, but liberal Reform Jews are sometimes called "Jewnitarians."

How Do You Like Your Blue-Eyed Boy Department

DEATH

The last religious taboo is death itself. Many and repulsive are the euphemisms we have coined for the activity of dying: "passing on," "going over," "buying the farm," "passing away," "kicking the bucket," "joining the angels," "biting the dust," "expiring," "departing," "breathing one's last," "negative patient care outcome," etc.

For the corpse itself we have coined more euphemisms: "the dear departed," "the deceased," "the earthly remains," "the loved one" . . .

But Mr. Death himself, being a *person,* has *nicknames.* He is known as: "The Grim Reaper," "The Great Leveler," "The Old Floorer," "The Last Roundup," "The Great Whipper," "The Big Jump," "Curtains," "Taps," "The End of the Line," "The Great Out," "The Debt of Nature," "The Big Sleep," "The Long Goodbye," "The Last Rattler," "The Last Post," "Kingdom Come" . . . and by W. C. Fields's perfect phrase, "The Man in the Shiny Pajamas."

Handles, Messiah Department

RELIGION & MYSTERY

The name that can be named is not the eternal name.

—Lao-Tzu

Chance is a nickname for Providence.

—Sebastien Chamfort, 1741–94

HOLY JOE   Joseph Stalin (Iosif Vissarionovich Dzhugashvili) *Soviet dictator*
THE POPE   Spencer Tracy *actor*
THE ARCHBISHOP   John W. McCormack *publisher*
THE RED DEAN   Archbishop Hewlett *(of Canterbury)*
THE BISHOP   Carmine De Sapio *mobster*
EPISCOPHAGOUS (BISHOP-EATING)   Thomas Henry Huxley *Darwinist paleon-tologist, aka "Darwin's Bulldog"*
DEACON   David Jones *football player* / Bill McKechnie, James White *baseball players*
THE GEORGIA DEACON   Theo "Tiger" Flowers *fighter*
PRIEST   Simon Nxawe *fighter*
THE HOODLUM PRIEST   (see Crime & Punishment)
THE VAULTING VICAR   Bob Richards *Olympic track star*
MOTHER   (see The Family)

THE SINGING NUN   Jeannine Deckers, aka "Soeur Sourire"—"Sister Smile"
  top 40 singer
THE SWIMMING NUN   Stella Taylor *athlete*
THE FLYING MONK   St. Joseph Copertino *levitator*
THE MAD MONK   Russ Meyer *baseball player*
MONK   Arthur Hazel *mellophone player*
THE FIGHTING PARSON   William G. Brownlow *politician*
WELSH PARSON   James J. Davis *Pennsylvania senator*
PREACHER   Elwin Rowe *pitcher*
THE PREACHER   (see "Canal Boy" James Garfield, U.S. Presidents)
REVEREND IKE   (Frederick Eikeren Koetter) *TV evangelist*
RABBI   Thomas Smith *philologist*
THE RABBI OF SWAT   Moe Solomon *baseball player*
SUPERJEW   Mike Epstein *baseball player*
THE LITTLE HEBREW   Abe Attell *featherweight champ 1901–12*
MOONIE   Lowell Miller *baseball player* / Keith Moon *onetime Who drummer*
THE EVANGELIST   Bill Sunday *pitcher*
THE MAHATMA   Wesley Branch Rickey *baseball exec*
PROPHET JONES   James F. Jones *faith healer*
DUMB PROPHET   (see Grover "The Buffalo Hangman" Cleveland, U.S. Presidents)
FATHER DIVINE   George Baker *minister, aka "God"*
THE IMMORTAL   Jose Azcue *baseball player*
THE MIRACLE MAN   George Stallings *baseball player*
WHISPERING JESUS   Adolph Zukor *chairman of the board, Paramount Studios*
DARLING OF THE GODS   Tallulah Bankhead *actress*
THE SCOURGE OF GOD   Attila *Hun*
LORD   (see Assumed Titles)
MOSES   Joe Shipley *pitcher*
GOLDEN RULE   Samuel Jones *factory owner*
ANGEL OF THE BATTLEFIELDS   Clara Barton *Red Cross founder*
THE PHANTOM ANGEL   Milton "Santa" Petrie *philanthropist, aka "Daddy Big*
  Bucks"
THE ANGEL OF DEATH   Josef Mengele *Nazi war criminal*
BLUE DEVIL   Eric Tipton *baseball player*
HELL'S DEVIL   Smedley D. "Old Gimlet Eye" Butler *major general, U.S. Marines*
ROBERT THE DEVIL   Robert I *father of "William the Conqueror" (William I)*
THE SEA DEVIL   Felix Luckner Von Graf *German naval commander, WWI*
IMP   Jim Begley *baseball player*
FATHER, SON   (see The Family)
THE SPIRIT   Mickey Davis *basketball player*
THE GALLOPING GHOST   Harold "Red" Grange *football immortal*
GHOST   Horace Greeley *journalist and politician, aka "Old White Hat"*

GHOST OF THE GHETTO   Sid Terris *fighter*
SPOOK   Forrest Jacobs, Bob Speake *baseball players*
SPOOKS   Wally Gerber *baseball player*
BOO   (see Ringers)
THE GHETTO WIZARD   Benny Leonard *fighter*
THE WELSH WIZARD   Lloyd George *British PM*
THE WIZARD OF MENLO PARK   (or OF THE WIRES) Thomas Alva Edison
    inventor
THE WIZARD OF OZ, OF OOZE   (see Cartoon & Other Literary Figures)
THE WIZARD OF TUSKEGEE   George Washington Carver *botanist, educator*
THE WIZARD OF WESTWOOD   John Wooden *basketball player, coach, aka "The
    India Rubber Man"*
MR. WIZARD   (Don Herbert) *television scientist*
WIZ   Ray Kremer *baseball player*
THE WITCH OF WALL STREET   Hetty Green *financier*
HOUDINI OF THE HARDWOOD   John Townsend *basketball player*
L'ANGELO MYSTERIOSO, MAESTRO MYSTERIOSO   George Harrison *Beatles
    pseudonyms*
MYSTERIOUS   Dave Mather *gunfighter*
MYSTERIOUS BILLY   Amos Smith *welterweight champ 1892–94*
THE LITTLE MAGICIAN   (see "Little Van" Matty Van Buren, U.S. Presidents)
MAGIC   Earvin Johnson *basketball player*
MAGIC DICK   Richard Salwitz *harmonica player*
MAGIC SAM   Sam Maghett *pop singer*
TRICKY DICK   (see "Tricky" Dick Nixon, U.S. Presidents)
TRICKY SAM   Joe Nanton *jazz trombonist*
LITTLE BOX OF TRICKS   Thomas "Pedlar" Palmer *fighter*
PRESTO   *how Jonathan Swift signed his letters to "Stella" (Hester Johnson)*
CHANGO   Erubey Carmona *fighter*
WHAMMY   Charles Douglas *pitcher*
STIMY   Henry L. Stimson *statesman, served 5 administrations*
STYMIE   Matthew Beard, Jr. *actor (Our Gang)*
BUNK   William Johnson *trumpeter*
SAM THE SHAM   Domingo Samudio *leader of the Pharoahs*
HOOEY LONG   (see "Kingfish," Assumed Titles)
LUCKY   Charles Luciano *criminal, aka "King of the Pimps"*
LUCKY LINDY   Charles "The Lone Eagle" Lindbergh *hero*
HARD LUCK   Henry Bruder *football player*
JINX   Eugenia Falkenberg *model, actress, pitchwoman*

11
NATURE BOYS

By Any Other Name Department

FLOWERS

Rose is a rose is a rose.

—Gertrude "Lovely" Stein

THE FLOWER   Guy Lafleur *hockey scoring champ*
THE LITTLE FLOWER[1]   Fiorello H. La Guardia *NYC reform mayor 1935–45*
THE ALABAMA BLOSSOM   Guy Morton *baseball player*
THE ORCHID MAN[2]   Georges Carpentier *light heavyweight champ 1920–22*
THE BLACK DAHLIA   Elizabeth Short *movie starlet & murder victim*
THE BLACK TULIP, LA TULIPE NOIRE (see "Pele," One-Name Wonders)
THE STEEL MAGNOLIA   Rosalynn Carter *first lady 1976–80*
THE JERSEY LILY[3]   Lillie Langtry (Emelie Le Breton) *actress 1853–1929*
THE ROSE   Sammy Rosenman *judge, politician*
CHRYSANTHEMUM   Joe Choynski *fighter*
BUTTERCUP   Louis Dickerson *outfielder 1878–85*
POPPY   Ray Davis *welterweight fighter*
DAISY   John A. Davis *pitcher 1884–85*
GARDENIA   Grover Whalen *businessman, politician, aka "The Gorgeous Greeter"*
GENERAL MUM   (see William "Tippecanoe" Harrison, U.S. Presidents)

1. The Flower, The Little Flower. Not so much nicknames as translations, but what the heck?
2. The Orchid Man. French-born Georges Carpentier won the European light heavyweight crown from "Bandsman" Rice in 1913, and the heavyweight title from "Bombardier" Billy Wells later that year. He then claimed the "white" heavyweight title by defeating England's "Gunboat" Smith in 1914. (Jack Johnson was then "black" heavyweight champ.) Postwar, in Jersey City, Carpentier took the inter-racial world light heavyweight crown from "Battling" Levinsky, (see Assorted Mayhem). In 1921, going for the Big One, he was KO'd in four by Jack Dempsey. Next year he lost his light heavyweight crown, in Paris, to "Battling" Siki.
3. The Jersey Lily. Her husband, Monsieur Langtry, was pleased to be cuckolded by "The Prince of Whales," Edward.

CORPORAL VIOLET   Napoleon "Little Boney" Bonaparte *aka "The Little Corporal"*
SWEET PEA   Roy Jefferson *football player*
SWEE' PEA[4]   Billy Strayhorn *musician, composer*
MISTLETOE POLITICIAN   (see "Little Van" Matty Van Buren, U.S. Presidents)
POISON IVY   Ivy Paul Andrews *pitcher 1931–38*
CACTUS   Clifford "Gaavy" Cravath *outfielder 1908–20*
CACTUS JACK   (see "Poker Face," Head to Toe [Faces])
DANDELION   Fred Pfeffer *baseball pitcher, manager 1884–94*
WEED   Alex Groza *basketball player*
SEED   Robert "Butch" Goring *hockey player*
JACK ROOT   (Janos Ruthaly) *first light heavyweight champ 1903*

I Hear Your Name and I'm Aflame Department

WOOD & FIRE

WOODY   Woodrow Guthrie *singer, songwriter* / Wayne Hayes *football coach* /
   Woodrow Herman *clarinet player* / "Doc" Wilson (see U.S. Presidents) / etc.
WOODY ALLEN   (Allen Konigsberg) *comedian, filmmaker*
WOODEN   Joe Nichols *clarinetist*
LUMBER   Joe Price *baseball player*
OLD HICKORY   (see Andy "Old Hickory" Jackson, U.S. Presidents)
PINE TOP   Clarence Smith *pianist*
DEADWOOD DICK   Richard Clarke *stagecoach driver*
TREE   John W. Addams *football player* / Wayne Rollins *basketball player*
BUSH   Bob Borkowski *outfielder*
STICK   Gene Michael *baseball coach*
WIELDER OF THE BIG STICK   (see "Bullmoose" Teddy Roosevelt, U.S. Presidents)
THE TWIG   Wayne Terwilliger *baseball player*
TWIGGY   (Leslie Hornby) *model, actress*
THE SPLENDID SPLINTER   Ted Williams *baseball great, aka "Teddy Ballgame"*
TOOTHPICK   Samuel Jones *pitcher, aka "Sad Sam"*
SLATS   Amory Gill *baseball coach*

Fire

MATCHES   Matt Kilroy *pitcher*
SPARKY   George Anderson *baseball manager* / Albert Lyle *pitcher*
FLASH   (see Movement)

4. Swee' Pea. It was Strayhorn, not "Duke," who wrote Ellington's theme song, "Take the A Train."

THE MEMPHIS FLASH   (see "The King," Assumed Titles)
FLAME   Lee Delhi *pitcher*
WILDFIRE   Harry Schulte *baseball player*
FIREBALL   Glenn Roberts *car racer*
FIREMAN   Joe Page *baseball player, aka "The Pitching Poet"*
SMOKE   Bill Herring *baseball player*
SMOKEY   William Robinson *singer* / Joe Wood *baseball player*
SMOKIN'   Joe Frazier *heavyweight champ*

Your Name Is Mud Department

WEATHER

STORMY WEATHERLY   Roy Weatherly *outfielder*
STORMIN'   Norm Van Lier *basketball player*
STORMIN' GORMAN   Gorman "Big Spike" Thomas *baseball player*
GALE STORM   (Josephine Cottle) *actress*
JET STREAM   James Smith *football player*
WINDY   John McCall, Ward Miller *baseball players*
BREEZY   Floyd Reid *football player* / George "Lefty" Winn *pitcher*
WHITECHAPEL WHIRLWIND   Jack "Kid" Berg (Judah Bergman) *junior welterweight champ 1930–31*
CYCLONE   William C. Haines *meteorologist* / Fred Taylor *hockey player* / Johnny Thompson *fighter*
THE PACIFIC CYCLONE   (see "Howlin' Mad," Attitudes)
THE ST. PAUL CYCLONE   Mike O'Dowd *middleweight champ 1917–20*
CYCLONE LOUIE   Vach Lewis *gangster*
HURRICANE   Ruben Carter *fighter* / Bob Hazle *baseball player* / Tommy Jackson *fighter*
THE HONDO HURRICANE   Clint Hartung *baseball player*
THE HOUSTON HURRICANE   A. J. Foyt *car racer*
THE TEXAS TORNADO   Jim Kern *baseball player*
THE TAN TORNADO, THE TAN THUNDERER, THE TAN THUNDERBOLT   (see "The Brown Bomber," Assorted Mayhem)
TWISTER   Paul Steinberg *basketball coach*
EARTHQUAKE, CHOCOLATE THUNDER   Daryl Dawkins *basketball player*
THUNDER MAKER   Howard Jones *football coach*
THUNDER   Andre Thornton *baseball player*
THUNDERCLAP   Andy Newman *British rock star*
THE ILLINOIS THUNDERBOLT   Ken Overlin *fighter*
LIGHTNIN'   Sam Hopkins *blues musician*

LOUISIANA LIGHTNING   Ron Guidry *baseball pitcher, aka "Gator"*
NIPPY   Vernal Jones *1st baseman*
FROSTY   Bill Duggleby *pitcher*
SNOW   Fred Snodgrass *outfielder*
THE BLOND BLIZZARD   Robert Fenimore *football player*
ICEBANKS   Charles W. Fairbanks *veep*
ICEBERG   (see "Chinese" Ben Harrison, U.S. Presidents)
ICEHOUSE   George Wilson *baseball player*
ICICLE   James Reeder *baseball player*
THE FOG   Fred Shero *hockey coach*
PHOG   Dr. Forrest Allen *basketball coach*
THE VELVET FOG   Mel Tormé *singer*
LANDSLIDE LYNDON   (see U.S. Presidents)
VOLCANO JONES   *pen name of Adrian Mitchell, aka "Apeman Mudgeon"*
MA RAINEY   (see The Family)
MR. SUNSHINE   Ernie "Mr. Cub" Banks *baseball Hall of Famer*
SUNNY   Martha von Bülow *socialite, victim*
SUNNY JIM   Jim Bottomley *baseball player* / James Sherman *Taft's veep* / A. A.
   Vandergrift *U.S. Marine general*
SUNNY JIM VALDARE   (James Mulligan) *vaudevillian*
SUNNYLAND SLIM   Albert Luandrew *singer, aka "Delta Joe"*
THE RAY   Benny "BG" Goodman, *aka "The King of Swing"*
SKY   Kenny Walker *basketball player*
SUNSET   Samuel S. Cox *politician*
SUNSET SAM   Sun Yat-sen *(to G.I.'s)*
TWILIGHT   Ed Killian *baseball player*
STARLIGHT   E. W. Rollins *19th-century heavyweight*
MOONLIGHT ACE   Fred Fussell *'20s pitcher*
GOVERNOR MOONBEAM   Jerry Brown *politician*
MUDDY WATERS   (McKinley Morganfield) *blues singer, musician*
RIVER   Reuben Reeves *musician*
RIO   River Phoenix *actor*
SWAMPY   Atley Donald *baseball player*
SWAMP BABY   Charlie Wilson *baseball player*
SWAMP RAT   (see Animals)
THE HUMAN WINDMILL   Harry Greb *middleweight champ 1923–26*
WINDMILL   Lauren Bacall (Betty Joan Perske) *actress, aka "The Look"*
FOGHORN   Forrest C. Allen *politician* / George "Doggie" Miller *baseball player,*
   aka "Calliope" / George Myatt *baseball player, manager, aka "Stud," "Mer-*
   cury"

12
NICKNACKS
(ODDS AND ENDS)

100 ONE-NAME WONDERS (A to Z)

An arbitrary list of celebrities known to us (often by their own choice) by one single solitary name. For our purposes, first names count ("Madonna" really *is* her first name), but last names don't (thus the exclusion of Haym *Topol,* Israeli actor; Tommy *Chong,* comedian; *Fabergé, Mantovani,* etc.).

Just imagine these mononymed folks meeting one another, in alphabetical order . . .

ADOLPHO	Adolpho Sardina	*Nancy's designer*
ANNABELLA	Suzanne Charpentier	*French film actress*
ANN-MARGRET	Ann-Margret Olsson	*Swedish-American actress, singer*
APOLLINAIRE	Wilhelm de Kostrowitzki	*French poet*
APOLLONIA	Patty Kotero	*backup singer*
ARMAN	Armand Fernandez	*French sculptor*
BASHO	Matsuo Munefusa	*Japanese haiku poet*
BENDIGO	William Thompson	*heavyweight champ 1839–40*
BLONDIN	J. F. de Gravelot	*French tightrope artist*
BOETHIUS	Anicius M. Severinus	*medieval philosopher*
BOTTICELLI[1]	Alessandro Filipepi	*Italian Renaissance painter*
BOWSER	John Baumann	*pop singer (Sha Na Na)*

1. "Botticelli" was actually the nickname of painter Alessandro's brother. It means "little barrel" and was presumably a slur.

BOZO	Frank Avruch	*TV clown*
BRICKTOP	Ada Beatrice Smith	*hostess, chanteuse*
BUDDHA	Guatama Siddhartha	*Enlightened One*
CALIGULA	Gaius Julius Caesar Germanicus	*Roman emperor*
CANDIDO	Candido Camero	*Cuban jazz musician*
CANTINFLAS	Mario Moreno Rèyes	*Mexican comic actor*
CAPUCINE	Germaine Lefebvre	*French model, actress*
CARAVAGGIO	Michelangelo Merisi	*Italian painter*
CASSANDRA	William Connor	*British columnist*
CHARO	Maria Rosario Malina	*singer, personality*
CHEECH	Richard Martin	*comedian (with Chong)*
CHER	Cherilyn Sarkisian LaPier	*singer, actress*
CHRISTO	Christoph Jaracheff	*sculptor*
CICERO[2]	Marcus Tullius	*Roman orator*
CLAUDE	Claude Gelee	*French landscape painter*
COLETTE	Sidonie-Gabrielle Colette	*French author*
DAGMAR	Virginia Egnor	*TV personality*
DANTE	Dante Alighieri	*Italian epic poet*
DION	Dion DiMucci	*pop singer (the Belmonts)*
DIVINE	Glen Milstead	*drag actor*
DONATELLO	Donato di Niccola Bardi	*Renaissance sculptor*
DONOVAN	Donovan Leitch	*British folk-rocker*
ERTÉ	Romaine de Tirtoff	*Russian designer*
FABIAN	Fabian Forte	*pop singer*
FELA	Ransome Kuti	*Nigerian superstar*
FERNANDEL[3]	Fernand Contandin	*French comic actor*
GENEVIEVE	Gingette Auger	*French chanteuse*
GENET	Janet Flanner	*journalist (The New Yorker)*
GERONIMO	Goyathly ("The Yawner")	*Sioux chief*
HALSTON	Roy Frowick	*designer*
HELOISE	Ponce Cruse	*hint-dispenser*
HERBLOCK	Herbert Block	*political cartoonist*
HILDEGARDE	Hildegarde Neff	*chanteuse*

2. "Cicero" means "wart," a reference to a growth on the nose of the longwinded Roman senator. "Cicero" was also the code name of Nazi spy Elias Basne, by the way.

3. Fernandel (Contandin) and fellow French actor Jean Gabin (whose real name was Jean-Alexis Moncorgé) once formed a production company together. Its title was a combination of their names, Mon Con, which means something naughty in French.

HOMER	Henry D. Haynes	*musician (with Jethro)*
HORACE	Quintus Horatius Flaccus	*Latin poet*
HOUDINI	Ehrich Weiss	*magician, escape artist*
JETHRO	Jethro Burns	*musician (with Homer)*
KIKI	Marie Prin	*French artists' model*
KOOL	Robert Bell	*pop singer (and the Gang)*
LEADBELLY	Huddie Ledbetter	*folk singer, convict*
LIBERACE	Wladiv Valentino	*pianist, showman*
LULU	Marie Lawrie	*British pop singer*
MADONNA	Madonna Ciccone	*pop star*
MANOLETE	Manuel Rodriguez y Sanchez	*Spanish matador*
MARGO	Marie Bolado Castilla y O' Donnell	*Mexican-American film star*
MEAT LOAF	Marvin Lee Aday	*pop singer*
MELANIE	Melanie Safka	*pop-folk singer*
MOEBIUS	Jean Girard	*French cartoonist*
MOLIÈRE	Jean Baptiste Poquelin	*French playwright*
MOLOTOV	V. M. Skryabin	*Soviet statesman*
MOONDOG	Louis Thomas Hardin	*composer*
MUHAMMAD	Abu al-Qasim Muhammad ibn Abd Allah ibn Abd al-Muttalib ibn Hashim	*Islam's prophet*
NADAR	Gaspard Felix Tournachon	*French pioneer photographer*
NERO	Lucius Domitus Ahenobarbus	*Roman emperor*
ODETTA	Odetta Gordon	*folk singer*
PARACELSUS	Theophrastus Bombast von Hohenheim	*Renaissance scientist, physician*
PELE[4]	Edson Donascimento	*Brazilian soccer star*
PHIZ[5]	Halbot Brown	*British illustrator*
PIGPEN	Ron McKernan	*drummer (Grateful Dead)*
PLATO[6]	Aristocles	*Greek philosopher*

---

4. Pele was Perola Negra ("Black Pearl") in Brazil, El Peligro ("The Threat") in Chile, La Tulipe Noire ("The Black Tulip") in France.

5. Phiz illustrated *The Pickwick Papers,* which Charles Dickens wrote under the pen-name "Boz."

6. "Plato," a nickname, is a reference to the peripatetic Athenian's broad shoulders.

PRINCE[7]	Prince Rogers Nelson	*rock star*
?	Rudy Martinez	*singer (and the Mysterians)*
REGINE	Regina Zylberberg	*nightclub owner, sycophant*
ROCHESTER	Eddie Anderson	*actor*
SABU	Sabu Dastagir	*actor, elephant boy*
SADE	Sade Adu	*Nigerian singer*
SPAIN	Manuel Rodriguez	*underground cartoonist*
SPANKY	George Emmet McFarland	*actor (with Our Gang)*
STENDHAL	Marie-Henri Beyle	*French novelist*
STING	Gordon Sumner	*British singer-actor*
SUZY	Aileen Mehle	*gossip columnist*
TAKI	Taki Theodoracopoulos	*gossip columnist*
TINTORETTO[8]	Jacobo Robusti	*Italian Renaissance painter*
TITIAN	Tiziano Vecellio	*Italian Renaissance painter*
TITO	Josip Broz	*Yugoslav marshal*
TOTÒ	Antonio de Curtis Gagliardi Ducas Comneno di Bisanzio	*Italian film actor*
TROTSKY	Lev Bronstein	*Soviet general, heretic*
TWIGGY	Leslie Hornby	*British model, actress*
ULTRA-VIOLET	Isabelle Collin-Dufresne	*Warhol superstar*
VANITY	Denise Matthews	*backup singer*
VERA-ELLEN	Vera-Ellen Rohe	*actress, dancer*
VERUSHKA	Vera Von Lehndorff	*fashion model*
VIVA	Susan Hoffman	*another Warhol superstar*
VOLTAIRE	François-Marie Arouet	*French satirist, philosopher*
WEEGEE	Arthur Fellig	*photographer*
XERXES[9]	Khshayarsha	*king of Persia (486– 465 B.C.)*
YOLANDA[10]	Emily Harris	*SLA kidnapper*
ZAG	Jerzy Zagorsky	*Soviet poet, playwright*

7. "Prince Rogers" was the stage name employed by the pop idol's father.
8. Tintoretto was the son of a dyer, hence the handle.
9. Xerxes is also called "Ahasuerus," in the Bible.
10. Yolanda. She helped Commander Cinque kidnap Tanya, remember?

Noms de Plume Department

LITERARY NICKNAMES

Homer is a perfect example of a *nom de plume*. Everybody knows that "Homer" did not compose the works attributed to him. They were obviously written by another blind old Greek with the same name . . .

Not only was "Homer" a nickname. Homer *invented* nicknames. Oh, all right, "epithets." Hector, son of Priam, was never just Hector, son of Priam, to Homer. He was Hector The-Horse-Tamer-with-Glancing-Helm. Cloud-Gathering Zeus was married to White-Armed Hera. Swift-Footed Achilles was beloved of Bright-Eyed Athene. And Odysseus was Crafty.

Double domes who are capable of distinguishing among static, dynamic, and transferred homeric epithets similarly can tell the difference between a *nom de plume* (pen name), a persona (first person narrator who is not the author), and "putative author" (the attribution of a work to another real or imagined writer). So Samuel Clemens, using the *nom de plume* Mark Twain, made Huckleberry Finn the putative author of his "Adventures." Are you following this? There will be a quiz.

Some authors use *noms de plume* out of legal necessity. Upon his release, ex-con William Sydney Porter preferred to start life anew as O. Henry (pen name indeed!). Clergyman-mathematician Charles Lutwidge Dodgson thought it advisable to publish his children's books as Lewis Carroll. Blacklisted screen writers (members of the Hollywood Ten) Alvah Bessie, Dalton Trumbo, Carl Foreman, Joseph Losey, and Howard Fast continued to turn out screenplays as Nedrick Young, Robert Rich, Derek Frey, Victor Hanbury, and E. V. Cunningham.

After Roscoe "Fatty" Arbuckle's scandalous misadventures with a soda-pop bottle, his on-screen credits read "Will B. Goode." Watergate mastermind E. Howard Hunt publishes cloak-and-dagger potboilers as John Baxter, Gordon Davis, and David St. John. Upon leaving Reading Gaol, Oscar Wilde published his "Ballad" as "C.3.3.3," which had been his prison number, then lived out his life under the pseudonym Sebastian Melmoth.

Other examples of writers obliged to use pen names include poor souls petitioning advice from newspaper sob sisters: "Desperate in Des Moines," "Puzzled in Peoria," and "Noisemaker." Curiously, their advisers and consolers often have pseudonyms, too: Ann Landers is Esther Pauline Friedman Lederer, and Abby van Buren is Pauline Esther Phillips.

A nasty novel concerning advice to the lovelorn columnists, *Miss*

Lonelyhearts, was written by Nathanael West (born Nathan Weinstein)—
"Pep" to his (ironic) pals.

A prolific author is sometimes obliged to take a pen name: John Burgess
Wilson (writing as Anthony Burgess) had to publish some of his novels as
Joseph Kell so as not to compete with himself for book shelf space and
reviews.

Because it is deemed unseemly for a Poet Laureate to write crime
novels, C. Day Lewis publishes his whodunnits as Nicholas Blake.

And in the days before women's lit was all the rage, female novelists
frequently assumed male pseudonyms in order to be taken seriously.
Armendine-Aurore-Lucile Dupin Dudevant called herself George Sand;
Mary Ann Evans, George Eliot. Karen Blixen published as Isak Dinesen, and
Acton, Currer, and Ellis Bell were Ann, Charlotte, and Emily Brontë.

Are You Kidding?

Satire, if performed properly, ought to result in violence. The object of
the satire should, if all goes well, make an attempt on his own life or that
of the author. For this reason, the art abounds with nicknames, pseudonyms, and *noms de plume.*

François-Marie Arouet signed himself Voltaire, usually, but in playful
moods attributed his unpleasantries to Le Docteur Goodheart, Une Belle
Dame, Rabin Akib, Catherine Vade, and Un Quaker. The optimistic philosopher Gottfried Wilhelm Leibniz he characterized as Doctor Pangloss.

Jonathan Swift scarcely signed his real name to anything. Even his
letters to Hester Johnson ("Stella") were attributed to "Presto" (Italian for
swift, get it?).

Gulliver's Travels were supposed, by the gullible, to have been written
by Lemuel Gulliver, merchant seaman. The seditious pamphlets Swift wrote
protesting English policy in Ireland were allegedly the work of one M. B.
Drapier, for whose identification and arrest a sizable reward was offered by
the authorities.

The Age of Reason was, if nothing else, an age of insulting literary
nicknames. Laureate John Dryden's rival poet Thomas Shadwell was lam-
pooned as Mac Flecknoe, aka "Shit." Lord Rochester dubbed the corpulent
Dryden "Poet Squab"; Alexander Pope nicknamed the succeeding laureate,
Colley Ciber, "The King of Dullness."

Beans, Eggs & Crumpets

As a creator of fictional nicknames, Pelham Grenville (P. G.) Wodehouse
—who himself answered to "Plum" and "Plummie"—was the master. The
impossibly upperclass and hopelessly twitty members of the Drones Club
(to which Bertram "Bertie" Wooster belonged) include Cyril "Barmy" Foth-
eringay-Phipps, Reginald "Pongo" Twistleton, Richard "Bingo" Little, Reginald "Kipper" Herring, Charles "Biffy" Biffen, The Reverend "Stinker"
Pinker, as well as miscellaneous Beefies, Bokos, and Corkies.

On one occasion, in *Psmith Journalist,* Wodehouse went so far as to
model a character, "Kid" Brady, on a real-life personage, "Kid" McCoy, a
middleweight champion (real name Norman Selby) who had KO'd 55 of his
105 opponents and murdered one of his ten wives. The outraged Kid chal-
lenged Plum to a bout of fisticuffs, which, fortunately, never took place.

More Than Somewhat

Damon Runyon (born Alfred Runyan) wrote stories of Broadway crap
shooters, bookies, showgirls, and lowlife—guys and dolls—featuring some
of the most spectacular nicknames ever. "Little" Isadore, "Milk Ear" Willie,
"Sky" (Obidiah) Masterson, "Joey Perhaps," "Brandy Bottle" Bates, "Feet"
Samuels, "Nicely Nicely," "The Louse Kid," Joe "The Blowfly," "Frying
Pan" Joe, "Hot Horse" Herbie, "Apple Annie," "Nathan Detroit," "Frankie
Ferocious," "Rosa Midnight," "Meyer Marmalade," "Big False Face," "Last
Card Louie," "Dream Street Rose," Sam "The Gonoph," "Brick" McCloskey,
and Hymie "Banjo Eyes" Weinstein. What's more, Runyon's heroes and
villains were usually based on real-life New York types with real-life
nicknames every bit as outrageous.

Angie "The Ox" is modeled after mobster Ciro Terranova, "The Arti-
choke King." "Regret" is a thinly disguised portrait of hitman Otto
"AbbaDabba" Berman. Dave "The Dude" is none other than Frank Costello,
"The Prime Minister," and his lady friend "Miss Missouri" Martin is Mary
Louise "Tex" Guinan, speakeasy operator to the stars. Harry "The Horse"
is Vincent "Mad Dog" Coll, and Armand "The Brain" Rosenthal was so
obviously Arnold "The Big Bankroll" Rothstein that the latter adopted "The
Brain" as an additional honorific.

Hip Handles

One of Runyon's greatest characters was "The Seldom Seen Kid," a
character notorious for his anonymity, and clearly an ancestor of William
Burroughs's "Subliminal Kid."

Burroughs, aka Bill Lee, is another chronicler of the underworld, and likewise peoples his fictions with nicknamed criminals. There's "Short Count" Tony, "Technical Tillie," "Uranium Willie," aka Willie "The Rat," aka "The Heavy Metal Kid," "Pantopon Rose," "Half-hanged Kelley," "The Paregoric Kid," and the notorious narc Salvador Hassan O'Leary, known as "Wrong Way Marv," "Blubber Wilson," "Finky Marv," "Wrongo Sal," "The Shoe Store Kid," and "The Musical Fruit."

The author's own nickname is "Bull," which was assigned to him by Jack Kerouac—in various Kerouac novels he is "Bull" Hubbard, "Bull" Dennison, and Frank "Bull" Carmody.

As for Kerouac (born Jean-Louis Kerouac) himself . . . his mother *"ma mère"* always called him "Ti-Jean." In his memoir-novels he called himself Sal Paradise, Jack Duloz, and Leo Percepied, but often signed personal letters "Jean-Louis Incogniteau." His pal Neal Cassidy is sometimes Dean Moriarity, and more often Cody Pomeray. Poet Allen Ginsberg appears in Ti-Jean's ouvre as Irvin Garden, Alvah Goldbook, Carlo Marx, and Leon Levinsky.

Where Credit Is Due

Because writing for the screen is at best a collaborative undertaking and at worst an exercise in promiscuous harlotry, many movie scenarios are pseudonymous. Even William Goldman, who claims to be proud of his craft, gave screenwriting honors for *Butch Cassidy and the Sundance Kid* to Robert Parker (which was Butch Cassidy's real name).

But pound-for pound (as the saying goes), the *noms-de-plume* championship of the century is held by screenwriter William Claude Dunkenfield, who began his artistic career as a juggler billed as Whitey "The Boy Wonder." He received screenplay credit (and opened bank accounts) under the following names:

Charles Bogle	Egbert Sousé
Otis Cribblecrobis	Cuthbert Twillie
Mahatma Kane Jeeves	Gus Winterbottom
Professor Quaile	Ambrose Woolfinger.

He appeared in his own cinematic masterpieces as just plain W. C. Fields.

That's Easy for You to Say Department

YAYAs

My name is Micha Micha but call me Toffey Tough.

—Anon

ACK-ACK   The Aluminum Company of America
BABA   Nestor Jiminez, Ivor Simmons *fighters*
BEBE   Charles Gregory Rebozo *Nixon's friend*
BEE BEE   Lee Richard *Chisox infielder*
BOBO   Alva Holloman, Norman Newsom *pitchers* / Carl Olson *middleweight champ 1953–55*
BOOM BOOM   (see Ringers)
BULLA BULLA   Ernie Davis *middleweight*
BYE BYE   Steve Balboni *1st baseman, slugger*
CHA CHA   Orlando "Baby Bull" Cepeda *1st baseman* / Jose Jimenez *Bolivian rebel*
CHI CHI   Juan Rodriguez *golfer*
CHOO-CHOO   (see Getting There)
COCO   Gabrielle Chanel *fashion designer* / Jose Laboy *Expos 3rd baseman*
COW COW   Charles Davenport *jazz pianist*
DADA   Idi Amin *deposed cannibal*
OLD DOB DOB   Sir William Dobbie *British general, WWII*
DODO   Doris Day *singer, actress* / Charles Dodgson[1] (Lewis Carroll) *author* / Michael Marmarosa *jazz pianist*
DUM DUM   Jose Luis Pacheco *middleweight*
FIFI   Fernanda Oscard *agent*
GEE GEE   Gus Getz, Jim Gleason *baseball players*
JAY JAY   James Johnson *jazz trombonist*
JO-JO   Joe Moore, Joyner White *outfielders*
JOHN JOHN   (see "Jackie O," The ABCs)
KIKI DEE   (Pauline Mathews) *pop singer*
KIKI[2]   Hazen Cuyler *outfielder*
LOCO LOCO   Ricardo Bennett *featherweight*
LULU   (Marie Lawrie) *British pop star*
MOMO   Sam Giancana *mobster, aka "Money"*
SEN-SEN   John P. J. Sensenderfer *old-time ball player*
TAP TAP   Elijah Makhatini *middleweight*
TY TY   Johnny Tyler *outfielder*
UBBO UBBO   Joe Hornung *outfielder 1879–90*

---

1. Dodo. Mathematician-photographer "Lewis Carroll" stammered when he attempted to pronounce his last name—except in the company of prepubescent girls.
2. Kiki. The Pirates Hall of Fame outfielder stammered *all* the time.

WAH WAH   Wallace Jones *football player*
YA YA   Y. A. Tittle *quarterback, aka "Bald Eagle"*
YEYE   Hector Hernandez *welterweight*
YO-YO   Pompeyo Davalillo *Senators shortshop 1953*
ZAZA   Erwin Harvey *pitcher-outfielder 1900–02*
ZSA ZSA³   Sari Gabor *celebrity*

You Can Call Me J . . . Department

THE ABCs

THE BIG A   Lew Alcindor (now Kareem Abdul Jabbar) *basketball player, noted for his "Sky Hook" shot* / Aqueduct Raceway *NY track*
DR. A   Al Silverstein *medical columnist*
AE   George Russell *Irish poet, novelist*
AuH₂O   Barry Goldwater *Arizona senator (while campaigning for president)*
MR. B   Billy Eckstine *singer*
WILLIE B   William B. Williams *NY radio personality*
B. G.   Benny Goodman *aka "The King of Swing," "The Ray"*
MR. C   Perry Como *singer, aka "Mr. Relaxed"*
KING OF THE HIGH C's   Luciano Pavarotti *opera star*
ERNIE D   Ernie DeGregorio *basketball player*
JOE D   Joe DiMaggio (see "Joltin'," Assorted Mayhem)
BIG D, DOUBLE D   Don Drysdale *Dodger pitcher*
BIG D   Dallas, Texas
E   Elvis Presley *(to the "Memphis Mafia")* (see "The King," Assumed Titles)
THE BIG E   Elgin Baylor, Elvin Hayes *basketball players* / Ernie Smith *fighter*
JOE E   Thurman Tucker *baseball player*
FDR   Franklin Delano Roosevelt *aka "W.P.A.-1 President," "Alphabet Soup-Kitcheneer" (see U.S. Presidents)*
FPA   Franklin P. Adams *columnist*
BIG G   John Gianelli *basketball player*
MR. G   Irv Gikofsky *NY TV weatherman*
G-MAN NO. 1   J. (John) Edgar Hoover *FBI chief*
THE G.O.M. (GRAND OLD MAN)   William Gladstone *British PM*
H. D.   Hilda Doolittle *imagist poet (nom de plume)*
DR. J   Julius Erving *basketball star*
JEB   (J)ames (E)well (B)rown Stuart *Confederacy commander, aka "Beauty"*
JFK   (see Jack Kennedy, U.S. Presidents; also see "Jackie O," next page)

---

3. Zsa Zsa. The oft-wed Hungarian-born actess fulfills Marshall McLuhan's definition of a celebrity: "Someone famous for being famous."

BIG K   Ted "Big Klu" Kluzewski *baseball player*

DR. K   Dwight Gooden *Mets pitcher ("K" is how you mark a strikeout on your scorecard)*

HENRY THE K   Henry "Superkraut" Kissinger *diplomat*

MURRAY THE K   Murray Kauffman *deejay, aka "The Fifth Beatle"*

K. B. GILDEN   *nom de plume of writing team Katya and Bert Gilden*

KO   Meyer Christner *'20s heavyweight*

L.A. (LITTLE AL)   Albert Bell *football player*

MR. LSD   Stanley Owsley *acid manufacturer*

THE BIG M   Frank Mahavolich *hockey star*

THE DIVINE MS. M   Bette Midler *actress, singer*

M MARK   Marsha Mark *editor, writer*

THE BIG O   Roy Orbison *singer* / Oscar Robertson *basketball player* / Otto Velez *1st baseman* / Montreal's Olympic Stadium

O. HENRY   (William Sydney Porter) *American short-story writer*

O. J.   Orenthal James Simpson, *aka "The Juice"*

O. K. HALL   Abraham Oakey "Elegant" Hall *the name with which the crooked New York mayor signed his checks*

JACKIE O   Jacqueline Kennedy Onassis *daughter of "Black Jack," JFK and Ari's wife, mother of John John*

TONY O   Tony Esposito *Black Hawk goalie, shutout whiz, brother of "Espo" (Phil)*

PDQ BACH   (Peter Schickele) *classical music parodist*

Q   Arthur Quiller-Couch *British author-critic*

ADMIRAL Q   *FDR's WWII code name*

HARRY S   Truman *"S" is the real middle name of "Give 'em Hell" Harry "The Haberdasher"*

BOOKER T   Booker T. Jones *leader of the MGs*

BIG T   Weldon "Jack" Teagarden *trombone player*

MR. T   Lawrence Tero *actor ("The A Team")*

T REX   Marc Bolan *British pop singer*

JOHNNY U   Johnny Unitas *quarterback*

GARY U.S. BONDS   Gary Bonds *American pop singer*

BILL W.   William Griffith Wilson *AA co-founder (as known to members)*

DOUBLE X   Jimmy "The Beast" Foxx *baseball Hall of Famer*

MALCOLM X   Malcolm Little *black separatist*

MISS X   A. Goodrich-Freer *psychic-author*

MR. X   Miller Barber *PGA VIP* / Russ Meyer *X-rated filmmaker* / Xavier Rescigno *pitcher*

BIG Z   Zelmo Beatty *basketball player*

There Goes Rhymin' Simon Department

RHYMERS

CHET THE JET   Chester Walker *basketball player*
CLYDE THE GLIDE   Clyde Drexler *basketball player*
DAVE THE RAVE   Dave Stallworth *basketball player*
DIEF THE CHIEF   John Diefenbaker *Canadian PM*
EARL THE PEARL   Earl Monroe *basketball player*
ELVIS THE PELVIS   (see "The King," Assumed Titles)
JAKE THE SNAKE   Jacques Plante *hockey goaltender*
MICK THE QUICK   Mickey "The Ambassador" Rivers *baseball player*
MIKE DE PIKE   Mike Heitler *criminal*
MURPH THE SURF   Jack Roland Murphy *burglar*
NATE THE SKATE   Nate "Tiny" Archibald *basketball player*
PHIL THE THRILL   Phil Sellers *basketball player*
ROGER THE DODGER   Roger Ward *car racer*
SAM THE SHAM   Domingo Samudio *musician*
STAN THE MAN   Stan Musial *baseball great*
TOM THE BOMB   Tom Tracy *Canadian football star*
WILT THE STILT   Wilt "The Big Dipper" Chamberlain *basketball player*
YUSSEL THE MUSCLE   Joe Jacobs *fighter, fight manager*
BRUCE THE MOUSE STRAUSS   *fighter*
BLUE LU   Lu Barker *musician*
DARLING CARLING   Carling Bassett *tennis player*
HANDY ANDY   Andy Pafko *baseball player*
JOLLY CHOLLY   Charlie Grimm *baseball player, aka "The Young Pretender"*
NEON LEON   Leon "Mess-Over" Spinx *heavyweight champ*
PUDDINGHEAD ED   Ed Battle *jazz musician*
RANDY ANDY   Prince Andrew, Duke of York *formerly "The Playboy Prince"*
SILLY BILLY   William IV *English monarch*
SLOW JOE   Joe Doyle *baseball player*
SMILER SCHUYLER   Schuyler Colfax *Grant's veep*
STARVIN' MARVIN   Marvin Freeman *baseball player*
STEADY EDDIE LOPAT   Edmund Lopatynski *baseball player*
STORMIN' GORMAN   Gorman "Big Spike" Thomas *baseball player*
TRICKY DICK   (see "Tricky" Dick Nixon, U.S. Presidents)
TURN 'EM LOOSE BRUCE   Bruce Wright *NY judge*
WEE BEA   Bea Booze *singer*
THE BULL UHLE   George Uhle *baseball player*
COCKY OCCY   Mark Occhilupo *surfer*
GOOBER ZUBER   William Zuber *baseball player*
HEINIE MEINE   Henry Meine *pitcher, aka "The Count of Luxembourg"*

HILLBILLY BILDILLI   Emil Bildilli *baseball player*
MILK SNATCHER THATCHER   Margaret Thatcher *British PM, aka "Attila the Hen," "The Iron Maiden"*
NIGHT TRAIN LANE   Richard Lane *football player*
RHYMIN' SIMON   Paul Simon *singer, songwriter*
SHUNT HUNT   James Hunt *British car racer*
SMASHER ASHER   Robert Asher *football player*
DOWNTOWN OLLIE BROWN   *baseball player*
JACK RABBIT JIM ABBITT   *football player*
LILTIN' MARTHA TILTON   *singer*
MEAN JOE GREENE   *Steelers lineman*
HER NIBS MISS GEORGIA GIBBS   *singer*
THE SINGING RAGE MISS PATTI PAGE   *singer*
WAVY GRAVY   (Hugh Romney) *hippie*
STILL BILL HILL   *baseball player*

I'm Mr. Lonely (Call Me Mr. Blue) Department

MISTERS

MR. ATTACK   Maxwell Taylor *U.S. general*
MR. BASKETBALL   Nat Holman *basketball Hall of Famer*
MR. BIG   Arnold Rothstein *criminal, aka "The Big Bankroll," "The (Big) Brain," "Czar of the Underworld"*
MR. BLUES   Wynonie Harris *singer*
MR. CHIPS   Bob Chipman *baseball pitcher*
MR. CLEAN   (see Gerry "Junie" Ford, U.S. Presidents)
MR. CUB   Ernie "Mr. Sunshine" Banks *Cubs baseball immortal*
MR. DEMOCRAT   Sam "Mr. Sam" Rayburn *Speaker of the House*
MR. DINGLEBERRY   Timothy Kay Dinsdale *Welsh author*
MR. DYNAMITE   James "Mr. Please Please" Brown *singer, aka "The Godfather of Soul," "Soul Brother No. 1," "The Hardest Working Man in Show Business"*
MR. ECONOMY   Harry "Curly" Byrd *Virginia senator*
MR. EXCITEMENT   Jackie Wilson *singer*
MR. 5 × 5   Jimmy Rushing *singer*
MR. GOALIE   Glen Hall *Chicago Black Hawk*
MR. GUITAR   Chet Atkins *guitarist*
MR. HOW-ABOUT-THAT   Mel Allen *sports announcer*
MR. IMPOSSIBLE   Brooks Robinson *Baltimore 3rd base immortal*
MR. INSIDE   Felix "Doc" Blanchard *football player*
MR. KENNETH   Kenneth Marlowe *society hairdresser*
MR. KNICKERS   Gene Sarazen *golfer*

MR. MAY   Dave Winfield *baseball player, thus slandered by the Yankee owner*

MR. MIKE   Michael O'Donoghue *writer*

MR. MOVES   Steve Boros *Padres manager, named by Graig Nettles for his frequent lineup changes*

MR. OCTOBER   Reggie Jackson *baseball immortal, for his post-season prowess*

MR. OUTSIDE   Glen W. Davis *football runningback*

MR. POPS   Arthur Fiedler *conductor (The Boston Pops)*

MR. REPUBLICAN   Robert A. Taft *politician, presidential candidate*

MR. SMITH   *incognito of king Louis-Philippe when he fled to Newhaven, 1848*

MR. TELEVISION   Milton "Uncle Miltie" Berle (Berlinger) *comedian*

MR. WARMTH   Don Rickles *insult comedian*

MR. WIZARD   Don Herbert *TV scientist*

MR. WONDERFUL   Sammy Davis, Jr. *entertainer*

MR. ZERO   Charlie Brimsek *hockey goalie (compare "Tony O," The ABCs)*

MR. B, MR. C, MR. G, MR. LSD, MR. T, MR. X   (see The ABCs)

MISTER   Reynaldo Snipes *heavyweight*

MASTER MELVIN   Mel Ott *baseball Hall of Famer*

MONSIEUR   Charles *French "citizen" king*

SEÑOR WENCES   Wenceslas Moreno *puppeteer, ventriloquist*

EL SEÑOR   Al Lopez *Detroit baseball immortal*

MISS PEGGY LEE   (Norma Egstrom) *singer*

MISS LILLIAN   Lillian Carter *first mother, Billy's mom*

MISS VICKY   Vicky May Budinger *married Tiny Tim on "The Tonight Show"*

MISS X   A. Goodrich-Freer *psychic-author*

THE DIVINE MISS SARAH   "Sassy" Vaughan *singer*

THE DIVINE MS. M   Bette Midler *singer, actress*

MADAME DAMALA   Sarah "The Divine" Bernhardt *actress*

YES MA'AM   William T. Sherman *Union general*

Sounds Like Department

RINGERS

BING   Harry Lillis Crosby *singer* / Edmund Miller *baseball player*

CHING   Ivan Johnson *hockey player*

PING   Frank Bodie *baseball player*

RING   Ringgold Wilmer Lardner *writer*

DING   Jay Darling *editorial cartoonist*

DING DONG   Bill Bell, Gary Bell *baseball players*

BUZZ   Edwin Aldrin *astronaut* / Burgess Meredith *actor* / Vern Miller *choreographer*

TWEET   Joe Walsh *baseball player*

TICK   Thomas Gray *trumpet player*
POP   (see The Family)
HOOT   Bob Gibson, Samuel Gibson *baseball players* / Edward Richard Gibson *cowboy actor*
TOOTS   John Hoffman *NY governor* / Bernard Shor *restaurateur* / Jean Thielmans *harmonica player*
SQUEAKY   Lynette Fromme *failed assassin, Manson girl* / Fred Valentine *baseball player*
BOOM BOOM   Walter Beck *pitcher* / Freddie Cannon (Freddie Picarilleo) *pop singer* / Bernie Geffrion *hockey player* / Ray Mancini *fighter*
YIP   E. Y. Harburg *songwriter*
WAHOO   Sam Crawford *baseball player*
EE-YAH   Hughie Jennings *baseball Hall of Famer*
WHIZ   Johnny Gee *pitcher*
SWISH   Bill Nicholson *outfielder*
ZONK   Larry Czonka *football player*
HI   Arthur Ladd *baseball player*
BOO   Bruce Smith *football player*
WHOA   Bill Phillips *baseball player*
WHOOP-LA   Will White *baseball player, "Deacon's" brother*
SONIC   Fred Smith *singer (with the MC5)*
NOISY   Johnny Kling *catcher*

Under the Spreading Family Tree the Village Smithy Stands Department

SMITHS

"Smith" means "metalworker" (goldsmith, blacksmith) and, by extension, craftsman (wordsmith, tunesmith). And way back when, those craftsmen were *very* prolific . . . because "Smith" is the most common family name in the English language, the most common in America, the most common in that phone book over there (unless you're in Hong Kong or Beijing—Chang is the most common in the world).

If your name is Smith, you'd better get yourself a nickname, to tell yourself apart. These Smiths did:

ALEXIS SMITH, Canadian-born singer-actress, née Gladys
AMERICA'S SWEETHEART, Canadian-born movie star, aka Mary Pickford, née Gladys Smith
BABYCAKES SMITH, football player Jerry T.
BALDY SMITH, Union general (with a full head of hair) William F.

BEETLE SMITH, WWII officer, aka "Bulldog"
BIG MAYBELLE, blues shouter born Mabel Louise Smith
BINGO SMITH, basketball player Bobby
BLACK RABBIT SMITH, Golden Gloves fighter and NFL guard Billy Ray
BLACKJACK, NFL lineman Henry E. Smith
BLUENOSE, Canadian east-coast poetess Norma Smith
BONECRUSHER SMITH, heavyweight champ James
BOO SMITH, running back Bruce P.
THE BORAX KING, manufacturer Francis Smith
BOSS JIM SMITH, New Jersey machine politician James
BROADWAY ALECK SMITH, baseball catcher Alexander Benjamin
BRICKTOP, singer and Parisian nightclub owner Ada Beatrice Queen Victoria Louisa
    Virginia du Conge Smith
BUBBA SMITH, NFL defensive end Charles A.
BUD SMITH, lightweight champ 1955–56 Wallace
BUFFALO BOB, Howdy Doody's human pal, Robert Smith
BUNTY SMITH, British woman golf pro Frances
BUSTER SMITH, jazz musician Henry
CATFISH SMITH, NFL defensive back Ralph
CADILLAC SMITH, NY politician William
CLIPPER SMITH, NFL veteran John
COLUMBIA GEORGE SMITH, pitcher George Allan
COTTON ED, U.S. representative from South Carolina Ellison Smith
DEAF SMITH, frontier scout and Old West legend Erasmus
DOC SMITH, sci-fi author, "Father of the Space Opera," E. E.
EMPRESS OF THE BLUES, immortal jazz singer Bessie Smith
FATHER SMITH, great British organ builder (1630–1708) Bernard
FIREBALL SMITH, pitcher Theolic
FLIGHT 45, pitcher Dave Smith
FUNNY PAPA SMITH, radio pop singer John T.
FUZZY SMITH, outfielder Alphonse
GERMANY SMITH, shortstop George J.
GUITAR BOOGIE, jazz musician Arthur Smith
GYPSY SMITH, frontier evangelist, the Reverend Rodney
THE HAPPY WARRIOR, NY governor, presidential candidate in 1928, Alfred E.
    Smith
HOOLEY SMITH, Montreal Maroons hockey star Reginald
HOWLIN' MAD SMITH, WWII U.S. Marine General Howland, aka "The Pacific
    Cyclone"
ICEBERG SMITH, Coast Guard Admiral Edward H.
JABBO SMITH, jazz trumpeter Cladys
JAY SILVERHEELS, the actor who played "Tonto," born Harold Smith
JETSTREAM SMITH, NFL fullback James

JIM BLUEJACKET, *nom de jeu* of pitcher James Smith
JINGLE MONEY SMITH, turn-of-the-century embezzler James
KANGAROO SMITH, now Zaid Abdul-Aziz, NBA forward Donald A.
KLONDIKE SMITH, pitcher with a brief career, Frederick
LEGS SMITH, musician Larry
LITTLE BILLY SMITH, British music hall performer William
LITTLE CLIPPER SMITH, football coach John P.
MARK, Andrew Smith, who with brother "Trade" (William) made the cough drops
    and appeared on the box.
MACHINE GUN MOLLY, Canadian bank robber and murderess Monica Smith
MIDGET SMITH, fighter William J.
MONK SMITH, jazz musician Lester
MOON OVER THE MOUNTAIN GIRL, singer and patriotic institution Kate Smith
MR. BASKETBALL, North Carolina coach Dean Smith
MR. SMITH, name under which exiled emperor Louis-Philippe traveled to Newhaven
MYSTERIOUS BILLY SMITH, welterweight champ 1892–94, Amos
NIG SMITH, ace pitcher (2 no-hitters) Frank Schmidt
OIL SMITH, catcher Earl
OLD SPEX, Confederate officer Francis Smith
ONE-LUNG SMITH, gambler and con man George
PHENOMENAL SMITH, self-effacing pseudonym of pitcher John Gammon
PHILOSOPHY SMITH, pontificating U.S. rep from Illinois Thomas V.
PIANO SMITH, rock musician and composer Huey
PIANO MOVER SMITH, husky baseball player Frank
PINE TOP SMITH, blues musician and composer Clarence
P. J. PROBY, American rock singer and English superstar James Smith
POP SMITH, 2nd baseman Charles
POP BOY SMITH, pitcher Clarence
PORK CHOP SMITH, jazz musician Jerome
QUEEN OF THE COWGIRLS, horse opera singer-actress Dale Evans, née Frances
    Smith
RABBI SMITH, philologist Thomas
RED SMITH, dean of American sportswriters, Timesman Walter
RIVERBOAT SMITH, pitcher Robert Walkup
SILENT SMITH, eccentric New York millionaire James H.
SILENT TOM SMITH, horse trainer Thomas
SILVERBAGS, speedball injecter Cathy Smith
SILVER-TONGUED SMITH, English Puritan preacher Henry
SILVER WILLIE SMITH, American politician William T.
SKYROCKET SMITH, 1st baseman Samuel
SMITH AND DALE, vaudevillians Joseph Seltzer and Charles Marks
THE SMITH OF SMITHS, British clergyman and renowned wit Sydney
SMOOCHIE SMITH, songwriter Jerry Lee

SNUFFY SMITH, hockey player named after the funny-pages character, Clinton
SOAPY SMITH, California con man and swindler Jefferson
SONIC SMITH, musician (with MC5) Fred
STEVIE SMITH, pen name of celebrated British poet Florence
STUFF SMITH, jazz violinist Hezekiah
SUGAR RAY ROBINSON, great welterweight and middleweight champ, born Walker
    Smith
SUPER GNAT, small but dangerous NFL halfback Noland Smith
TAL SMITH, jazz musician Talmadge
TRADER HORN, British explorer and adventurer Alfred E. Smith
VITAMIN T, NFL halfback Verda Smith
WATERTIGHT SMITH, Michigan senator William A., who wondered, during the
    hearings on the Titanic tragedy, why the passengers didn't go below to the
    "watertight" compartments
WHISPERING JACK SMITH, country singer John
WHISPERING SMITH, pop singer Mose
WHISTLING BOB SMITH, horse trainer Robert A.
WIFFI SMITH, British woman golfer Margaret
WILLIE THE LION SMITH, jazz piano master William Henry Joseph Berthol
    Bonaparte Berthloff
WONDERFUL SMITH, jazz musician Floyd
WONDERFUL WILLIE SMITH, outfielder Willie
WOLFMAN JACK, growling deejay William Smith
Z. Z. SMITH, author David Westheimer

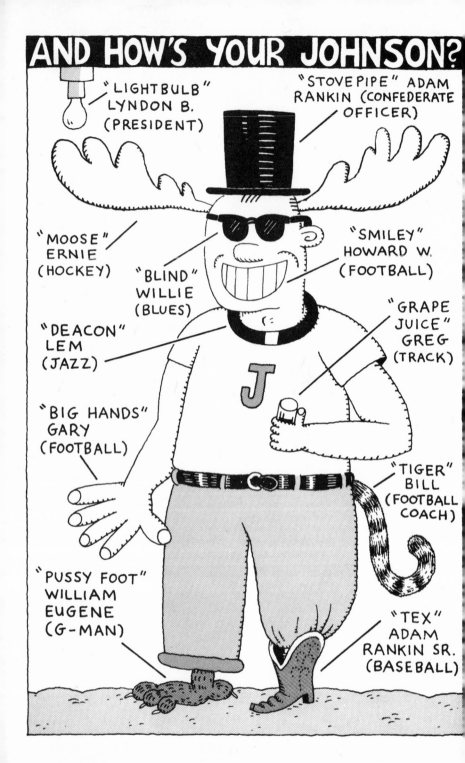